The Wacky World of Laws: Second Edition

A Detailed Look At Some Of The Strange Laws And Court Cases That Exist In The United States And Other Parts Of The World

By
Jeff Isaac, "The Lawyer in Blue Jeans" and
Attorney Justin Isaac

The Wacky World Of Laws: 2nd Edition

Wacky Laws From Around The World: A Detailed Look At Some Of The Strange Laws And Court Cases That Exist In The United States And Other Parts Of The World, By Jeff Isaac, "The Lawyer in Blue Jeans" and Attorney Justin Isaac

Published by Lawyer in Blue Jeans, Inc.
3990 Old Town Ave., Ste. A-103
San Diego, CA 92110
www.lawyerinbluejeans.com

Copyright © 2020 by Lawyer In Blue Jeans Group
Manufactured in the United States of America.
ISBN: 9798587678453

The Wacky World Of Laws: 2nd Edition

No part of this publication may be reproduced or distributed in any form or by any means, or stored in a database or retrieval system, without the prior written permission of the publisher.

Disclaimer of responsibility: The publisher and the author make no representations or warranties with respect to the accuracy or completeness of the contents of this work and specifically disclaim all warranties, including without limitation warranties of fitness for a particular purpose. No warranty may be credited or extended by sales or promotional materials. The advice and strategies contained herein may not be suitable for every situation.

This work is sold with the understanding that the publisher is not engaged in rendering legal, accounting, or other professional services. If professional assistance is required, the services of a competent professional person should be sought. Neither the publisher, or the authors, shall be liable for damages arising here from.

The fact that an organization or website is referred to in this work as a citation and/or a potential source of further information does not mean that the author or the publisher endorses the information the organization or website may provide or recommendations it may make. Further, readers should be aware that internet websites listed in this work may have changed or disappeared between when this work was written and when it is read.

Special thanks to Attorney Sarah Rush, for assistance with formatting and editing.

AUTHOR'S NOTE

Since I was a teenager, blue jeans were a standard dress code in my life. Little did I know that it would consume me and become a central component of my purpose throughout my career. To be clear, I have always been an advocate of doing things in a simple, yet efficient way, especially in my work.

When I started my legal career in 1976, I felt that I should act like a lawyer, dress like a lawyer, and go about my business in a way that was typically expected by society. It took representing thousands of clients, and hundreds of other legal efforts, for me to discover I needed something different. It was then that I realized perhaps the standard method used by everyone else in the past, was not the best way for me to replicate success in my own legal career. At this time, the "Blue Jeans" approach was founded; focusing on doing things my way, and not the stereotypical way which lawyers were expected to conduct business.

As if to cement this new way of thinking, I was referred to as "the Lawyer in Blue Jeans" on my radio show on 760 KFMB in San Diego beginning in the year 2000. It caught on like wildfire and has been both my brand and my passion since then.

Throughout the years, I have often been asked to define this concept that has become my way of life. The simplest way to define it is: "Blue Jeans Law" is my perception of how a lawyer should practice the art of law. That is to say, we should talk in common-sense English (not legalese), not talk down to our clients, and we should find the easiest, most-efficient way to take care of the client's legal needs.

In today's world, the public deserves to be represented by an attorney who could relate to each individual. Clients have needs, wants, emotions, and passions. Clearly, the old way of practicing traditional law doesn't respect these human characteristics. The "Blue Jeans" way demands that lawyers act professionally, yet with compassion and integrity. Lawyers should help their clients, not just blindly practice law.

During thousands of radio shows and television appearances (including local TV shows, spots on national networks like CNN, presentations on the Today Show, Fox and Friends, MSNBC, and so many others), I used this new way of thinking to provide legal commentary in an atmosphere that was light and comfortable. I believe this has helped foster an atmosphere of trust with clients and listeners who do not get the impression that I am trying to walk circles around them with confusing legal jargon.

Because of its unique and humorous content, the Wacky Law of the Day, became a popular feature on my radio show and during TV appearances. So many of these strange legislative attempts make you wonder what our law makers had in mind when they created such crazy legislation. With this in mind, this book attempts to give the public a laugh-out-loud look at some of the weird laws that have been written through the years.

This lighter side of law, provides the reader with great insight on the history of laws in the United States and the rest of the world. While reading this book, you will be amazed at how these laws have evolved over time. Some of them (quite a few are still in place) might even prompt you to ask yourself how the heck could anyone have composed these laws in the first place.

In all seriousness, these laws are somewhat reflective of our society, and should provide a reality check for our legislators when it is time to make legislative changes.

We invite you to immerse yourself in the "Blue Jeans" approach and be entertained by these wacky laws. If nothing more, you will have something clever and funny to share with friends and neighbors at your next event. I hope you enjoy what we have put together, and may you always be able to look at the lighter side of life!

Cheers!

Jeff Isaac
"The Lawyer in Blue Jeans"
October 2020

INTRODUCTION

Throughout history, legislatures have addressed such weighty issues as war, peace, taxes, slavery, and freedom. Unfortunately, they have also spent their time pondering such matters as what vermin should be considered the state insect, or if it should be legal to sing in a public place while in a bathing suit.

Some wacky laws actually had good reasoning behind them when they were created. As time went by, their reason for being slowly diminished and they became comical. Other laws never made much sense in the first place. Some wacky laws were based on court rulings. In legal circles, these are known as "case law".

An occasional wacky law was written because someone actually did the thing which the law now prohibits. In these cases, local authorities might have asked for legislative help in preventing anyone from repeating the offense in the future. District Attorneys will tell you it is easier to get a conviction for violating a very specific law.

Quite often, local councils and state legislatures have little interest or time to repeal old (and now wacky) laws. Without knowing a good reason why these laws were initially passed, legislatures are afraid they might alter some long held legal standard which could change the world as they know it. For example, a city park might have been deeded to a town with the provision that nobody over 12 years of age ever wear a red cap in the park. Perhaps the person giving the land to the city was beat up by hoodlums wearing red hats. One of the provisions of the deed could be that if the law was ever repealed, the land would revert to the heirs of the person who gave the land to the city. For that reason, many wacky laws might remain in effect out of fear.

The Wacky World Of Laws: 2nd Edition

Some wacky laws are merely urban myths. They have been repeated so many times that they have become accepted as truth. One such wacky law says it is illegal to count out loud backwards in hexadecimals in a certain California city. City officials have stated that no such law has ever existed in that town. The story probably started as a joke which was repeated so many times that it changed into a "true story", instead of a joke.

Other well-known "wacky laws" may never have actually been a specific, real law, even though doing what they prohibit could get you into trouble. For example, a wacky law seen on the internet says it is illegal to walk your pet giraffe without a leash. In fact, the actual law says it is illegal to walk "any pet" without a leash. So, walking a pet giraffe would, indeed, be illegal. Yet, no such law specifically prohibiting the walking of a giraffe actually exists. We have included many such "wacky laws" in this book.

In some cases, we have attempted to list the actual wacky law as it is written. In those cases, we have tried to quote the specific section involved, as it is written. If you are not familiar with "legalese", you can understand how some of these laws can get passed. Not many people can understand what they actually say, or what they were originally intended to mean. We have also posted a few wacky cases. In each case, someone actually did something wacky, which resulted in a lawsuit. It seemed appropriate to post these events in here as well.

Finally, when in doubt about any wacky law where you live, we recommend contacting your local authorities to check a law's veracity or if it is enforced. We also recommend keeping that pet giraffe on a leash. You never know.....

TABLE OF CONTENTS

AUTHOR'S NOTE 4
INTRODUCTION 7
ALABAMA 12
ALASKA 18
ARIZONA 21
ARKANSAS 25
CALIFORNIA 28
COLORADO 46
CONNECTICUT 51
DELAWARE 53
DISTRICT OF COLUMBIA 56
FLORIDA 57
GEORGIA 64
HAWAII 70
IDAHO 71
ILLINOIS 73
INDIANA 79
IOWA 83
KANSAS 86
KENTUCKY 90
LOUISIANA 92

MAINE	96
MARYLAND	98
MASSACHUSETTS	101
MICHIGAN	106
MINNESOTA	109
MISSISSIPPI	112
MISSOURI	115
MONTANA	118
NEBRASKA	121
NEVADA	123
NEW HAMPSHIRE	125
NEW JERSEY	126
NEW MEXICO	131
NEW YORK	132
NORTH CAROLINA	136
NORTH DAKOTA	140
OHIO	141
OKLAHOMA	145
OREGON	148
PENNSYLVANIA	152
RHODE ISLAND	155
SOUTH CAROLINA	157
SOUTH DAKOTA	161
TENNESSEE	162

TEXAS	166
UTAH	172
VERMONT	175
VIRGINIA	176
WASHINGTON	179
WEST VIRGINIA	183
WISCONSIN	185
WYOMING	188
FEDERAL LAW	190
INTERNATIONAL LAW	192
ABOUT THE AUTHORS	205

ALABAMA

Statewide:

- The Alabama constitution is the longest constitution in the world. According to experts, it is longer than the Bible or Moby Dick.

- It is illegal to modify the appearance of a mule or a horse's teeth in order to make them appear younger.

- You may not have an ice cream cone in your back pocket at any time.

- It is illegal to engage in bear wrestling, or to alter a bear so it can participate in a wrestling match. *Actual law: Section 13A-12-5 Unlawful bear exploitation; penalties. (a) A person commits the offense of unlawful bear exploitation if he or she knowingly does any one of the following: (1) Promotes, engages in, or is employed at a bear wrestling match. (2) Receives money for the admission of another person to a place kept for bear wrestling. (3) Sells, purchases, possesses, or trains a bear for bear wrestling. (4) For purposes of exploitation, subjects a bear to surgical alteration in any form, including, but not limited to, declawing, tooth removal, and severing tendons. (b) Unlawful bear exploitation is a Class B felony and is punishable as provided by law. (c) Upon the arrest of any person for violating this section, the arresting law enforcement officer, conservation officer, or animal control officer shall have authority to seize and take custody of any bear in the possession of the arrested person. (d) Upon the conviction of any person for violating the provisions of this section, any court of competent jurisdiction shall have authority to order the forfeiture by the convicted person of any bear, the use of which was the basis of the conviction. Any bears ordered forfeited under this section shall be placed in the custody of a humane shelter, a society that is incorporated for the prevention of cruelty to animals, or the state Department of Conservation and Natural Resources. (e) In addition to the fines, penalties, and forfeitures imposed under this section, the court may require the defendant to make restitution to the state, any of its political subdivisions, or a humane shelter or a society that is incorporated for the prevention of cruelty to animals for housing, feeding, or providing medical treatment to bears used for unlawful wrestling.*

- Anyone operating a motor vehicle cannot be blindfolded.

- It is illegal to wear a fake mustache in church which causes people to laugh.

- Before cars first appeared, it was illegal to open an umbrella on the street because it might startle a horse.

- You cannot force your child to play cards on a Sunday.

- Any person who compels his child, apprentice or servant to perform any labor on Sunday, except the customary domestic duties of daily necessity or comfort, or works of charity or who engages in shooting, hunting, gaming, card playing or racing on that day, or who, being a merchant or shopkeeper, druggist excepted, keeps open store on Sunday, shall be fined not less than $10.00 nor more than $100.00, and may also be imprisoned in the county jail, or sentenced to hard labor for the county, for not more than three months. However, the provisions of this section shall not apply to the operation of railroads, airlines, bus lines, communications, public utilities or steamboats or other vessels navigating the waters of this state, or to any manufacturing establishment which is required to be kept in constant operation, or to the sale of gasoline or other motor fuels or motor oils. Nor shall this section prohibit the sale of newspapers, or the operation of newsstands, or automobile repair shops, florist shops, fruit stands, ice cream shops or parlors, lunch stands or restaurants, delicatessens or plants engaged in the manufacture or sale of ice; provided, that such business establishments are not operated in conjunction with some other kind or type of business which is prohibited by this section.

- It is illegal to pretend to be a priest or a rabbi. *Actual Law: Whoever, being in a public place, fraudulently pretends by garb or outward array to be a minister of any religion, or nun, priest, rabbi or other member of the clergy, is guilty of a misdemeanor and, upon conviction, shall be punished by a fine not exceeding $500.00 or confinement in the county jail for not more than one year, or by both such fine and imprisonment. (Acts 1965, 1st Ex. sess., No. 273, p. 381; Code 1975, §13-4-99.)*

- Children born from an incestuous marriage are 'legitimate.' *Actual Law: Section 30-1-3 Issue of incestuous marriages not deemed illegitimate. The issue of any incestuous marriage, before the same is annulled, shall not be deemed illegitimate.*

- It is illegal to maim yourself in order to get charity of to escape your civic or military duties. *Actual Law: Every person who, with design to disable himself from performing a legal duty, existing or anticipated, shall inflict upon himself an injury whereby he is so disabled and every person who shall so injure himself with intent to avail himself of such injury to excite sympathy or to obtain alms or some charitable relief shall be guilty of a felony. (Code 1923, §4941; Code 1940, T. 14, §357; Code 1975, §13-1-6.)*

- You only get five minutes to vote according to state law.

- You can pick your nose while driving, but you cannot flick what you find out the window.

- In counties having populations of not less than 56,500 nor more than 59,000, according to the 1970 or any subsequent federal decennial census, domino games shall be lawful in billiard rooms or other rooms in which billiard tables are located. *A copy of the legislation can be seen here: http://www.legislature.state.al.us/CodeofAlabama/1975/34-6-12.htm*

Anniston:

- Blue jeans are not allowed on Noble Street.

Auburn:

- It is illegal to spit on the floor while you are in a church or a bus. Actual Law: It is unlawful for any person to spit upon the sidewalks, or upon the floors of places of worship, buses, public halls, theaters or other public places. (Ord. 63A 3-12, 1977)

- Riding a bicycle to a grocery or convenience store is forbidden.

Brewton:

- Traveling on city streets in a motorboat is not allowed.

Lee County:

- The selling of peanuts is prohibited after sunset.

Mobile:

- Women are not allowed to wear sharp high heel shoes. This is one of those laws that made some sense when it was passed. Several women wearing these types of shoes got them stuck in the city sewer gratings.

- There is no howling or hooting at women allowed. During World War II, lots of military men and ship builders came through Mobile. Their constant "howls" and "hoots" so antagonized the female population, a law was passed outlawing it.

- You cannot be a fortune-teller without getting a license. They could have predicted this, right? *Actual law: Sec. 23-21. Required. It shall be unlawful for any fortuneteller, as defined in section 23-1, to practice fortunetelling within the city or its police jurisdiction, without first obtaining a permit therefor in compliance with the provisions of this chapter.*

- Silly String & "Snap Pop" firecrackers are not allowed in Mobile. *Actual Law: Sec. 39-15. "Spray string," "snap pops," or similar matter or substances are prohibited. It shall be unlawful and an offense against the city for any person to have in his/her possession, keep, store, use, manufacture, sell, offer for sale, give away or handle any "spray string," "snap pops," or other matter or substances similar thereto, within the city within its police jurisdiction.*

- Spitting is illegal. *Actual Law: Sec. 39-76. Spitting or throwing fruit skins, etc., on sidewalks. No person shall spit or throw fruit skins, parings or peelings upon any sidewalk in the city or upon the floor of any bus operated within the city or in any public elevator, public building, public theater or public hall or upon any walkway in any public park in the city.*

- Possession of confetti is illegal. *Actual Law: Sec. 39-77. Use, sale, etc., of confetti. It shall be unlawful and an offense against the city for any person to have in possession, keep, store, use, manufacture, sell, offer for sale, give away or handle any confetti or other substance or matters similar thereto, but not serpentine, within the city or within its police jurisdiction.*

• You cannot take a bath in any of Mobile's city fountains.

• You can't sell stink balls or funk balls in Mobile. *Actual law: Sec. 39-81. Stink or funk balls. It shall be unlawful to sell, dispose of, give away or use within the city or its police jurisdiction articles known as stink balls or funk balls or anything of like nature, by whatever name known or called, the purpose of which is to create disagreeable odors to the great discomfort of persons coming in contact therewith.*

• "Lewd dresses" cannot be worn in public by women. *Actual law: Sec.39-112. Same--indecent dress, etc. It shall be unlawful for any person to appear in any public place in a state of nudity or indecent or lewd dress, or make an indecent exposure of his person, or to perform or commit any indecent act.*

• Eating pebbles from composition roofs is prohibited for pigeons.

Ryan Crossroads:

• A minister has the right to make a woman eating peanuts leave his church while services are going on.

ALASKA

Statewide:

• Moose are the subject of many laws in Alaska. According to some sources, it is both illegal to look closely at a moose from an airplane, or to push a live one out of an airplane.

• It is also illegal to whisper in someone's ear while they are moose hunting.

• Public places which preserve scenic vista get "bonus points." *Actual Law: 04 CBJAC 040.010 Scenic vistas. (a) Policy. Development which is designed and sited on land in such a way as to preserve scenic vistas visible from public places may be awarded bonus points.*

• While it is legal to shoot a bear (with a license or when fearing for your life), it is illegal to wake up a sleeping bear in order to take its picture.

• It is against the law to sell stun guns to children.

Anchorage:

• Tying your pet dog to the roof of your car is illegal. *Actual law: 9.36.150 Carrying animals on outside of vehicle. No person driving a motor vehicle shall transport any animal in the back of the vehicle in a space intended for any load on the vehicle on a street unless the space is enclosed or has side and tail walls to a height of at least 46 inches extending vertically from the floor, or the animal is cross tethered to the vehicle, or is protected by a secured container or cage, in a manner which will prevent the animal from being thrown, falling or jumping from the vehicle.*

Fairbanks:

- Here is another moose-related law. It is illegal to give a moose any alcoholic beverages.

- It is illegal to blow a horn in a manner that disrupts the peace in this town.

Juneau:

- If you own a flamingo or an aardvark, you cannot take them into a restaurant or a barbershop. *Actual law: 36.25.010 Prohibited; responsibility of animal owner. No owner of any animal or person having control of any animal shall allow such animal to enter upon any public premises where food for human consumption is sold, processed stored or consumed or to enter into any barber shops or establishments for the practice of hairdressing or beauty culture.*

- Dog grooming is illegal here.

Nome:

- Don't buy your child a bow and arrow set for Christmas. It could get you arrested. *Actual law: 13.25.050 Possession of air guns and similar devices. (a) No person shall have in his or her physical possession, nor shall discharge, an air gun, bow and arrow, or slingshot within the city. (b) The prohibitions of subsection (a) of this section do not apply to possession or discharging in authorized locations, or to transporting along a direct course between authorized locations, provided the device is not loaded while in route. (c) As used in this section: (1) "Air gun" means a BB gun, pellet gun or similar device which launches a projectile upon the release of compressed gas; and (2) "Authorized locations" means and includes occupied residences, operational vehicles, premises in which such devices are sold or displayed, and facilities designed for indoor charges.*

ARIZONA

Statewide:

• Not only is it illegal to sell illegal drugs, it is against the law to sell fake illegal drugs. *Actual law: 13-3453. Manufacture or distribution of imitation controlled substance; prohibited acts; classification - It is unlawful for a person to manufacture, distribute or possess with intent to distribute an imitation controlled substance.*

• This law is a subject of some contention. However, it is widely circulated that it is illegal to hunt camels in Arizona. It is speculated this was based on the camels that thrived for a while after the Army abandoned them in the desert. The Army had experimented with them for a while as pack animals just after the Civil War. When the experiment was dropped, the camels were set free.

• Many states have laws which make it against the law to deface the American Flag. In Arizona, it is illegal to place any mark on any flag which could incite others to take action against you. *Actual law: 13-3703. Abuse of venerated objects; classification -A. A person commits abuse of venerated objects by intentionally: 1. Desecrating any public monument, memorial or property of a public park; or 2. In any manner likely to provoke immediate physical retaliation: (a) Exhibiting or displaying, placing or causing to be placed any word, figure, mark, picture, design, drawing or advertisement of any nature upon a flag or exposing or causing to be exposed to public view a flag upon which there is printed, painted or otherwise produced or to which there is attached, appended or annexed any word, figure, mark, picture, design, drawing or advertisement; or (b) Exposing to public view, manufacturing, selling, offering to sell, giving or having in possession for any purpose any article of merchandise or receptacle for holding or carrying merchandise upon or to which there is printed, painted, placed or attached any flag in order to advertise, call attention to, decorate, mark or distinguish the article or substance; or (c) Casting contempt upon, mutilating, defacing, defiling, burning, trampling or otherwise dishonoring or causing to bring dishonor upon a flag.*

Glendale:

- Who knows why, but backing up your car can get you in trouble in certain parts of Glendale.

Globe:

- At one time, it was illegal to play cards.

- Two dildos in one house is acceptable, but any more than two is against the law.

Hackberry:

- On Sundays, women cannot eat raw onions while drinking buttermilk.

Hayden:

- While within the city limits of Hayden, bullfrogs or cottontail rabbits cannot be "disturbed."

Mesa:

- Long before the modern prohibitions against smoking in public buildings, it was determined that smokers had to have a Class 12 Liquor license to be able to smoke within 15 feet of a public place.

Mohave County:

- Anyone caught stealing soap must use it until it's all used up.

Nogales:

- Perhaps the mayor's daughter was scared by a man without a belt. Whatever the reason, wearing suspenders was deemed illegal in Nogales.

Phoenix:

- It seems obvious, but the law here says that every man who enters the city limits must be wearing pants.

Prescott:

- Even though it is a part of the Wild West, it is still illegal to ride a horse up the stairs of the county courthouse.

Quartzite:

- City leaders in this town were very concerned about maintaining a high moral climate for pregnant women, children and Indians. "Lest they acquire a taste for gambling" it was illegal to play cards with any of them.

Tombstone:

- While it might be cute for a youngster to have a missing tooth, this town made it illegal for anyone 18 or older to have more than one missing tooth showing when they smiled.

Tucson:

- Beware women libbers, it is illegal for women in Tucson to wear pants.

ARKANSAS

Statewide:

- Women who teach school cannot "bob their hair" if they expect to get a raise in salary.

- Bathtubs are not the proper place to raise an alligator.

- Oral sex is considered to be sodomy.

- To prohibit the improper pronunciation of the great state of Arkansas' name, a law was passed requiring that while you are in the state it must be pronounced "Ar-kan-saw."

- Perhaps fearing a flood, the state legislature passed a law that the Arkansas River can rise no higher than the Main Street Bridge in the state capital of Little Rock.

- Your dog better be able to tell time, because it is not allowed to bark after 6 PM.

- A man can legally beat his wife, but not more than once a month.

- Peeking in a window can get you into all kinds of trouble, even if it is only to watch an election. *Section 4761, Pope's Digest:* "No person shall be permitted under any pretext whatever, to come nearer than fifty feet of any door or window of any polling room, from the opening of the polls until the completion of the count and the certification of the returns."

Little Rock:

The Wacky World Of Laws: 2nd Edition

- You can't walk your pet in this town.

- Flirtation between men and women on the streets of Little Rock may result in a 30-day jail term.

- It is unlawful to walk one's cow down Main Street after 1:00 PM on Sunday.

- Honking a car horn at a sandwich shop is illegal after 9 PM.

- It's illegal to yell at your kids, or for your mother-in-law to yell at you at a drive-in restaurant. And don't even think about honking your horn after 9 PM. *Actual law: -Little Rock City Code Sec. 18-53 & 54. Conduct in drive-in restaurants. (a) In this section "drive-in restaurant" means any restaurant where meals, sandwiches, ice cream, or other food, is served directly to or is permitted to be consumed by patrons in automobiles, motorcycles or other vehicles parked on the premises. (b) It shall be unlawful for any person while on or adjacent to the premises of a drive-in restaurant to race the motor of any car, to suddenly start or stop any car, or to make or cause to be made, any other loud or unseemly noise. It shall be unlawful for any other person parked on the premises of a drive-in restaurant, to blow or cause to be blown any automobile horn or motorcycle horn at any time while parked. (c) It shall be unlawful for any patron or other person on the premises of a drive-in restaurant to drink any beer, unless purchased on the premises. It shall be unlawful for any patron or other person on the premises of a drive-in restaurant to create a disturbance or a breach of the peace in any way whatsoever, including but not limited to loud and offensive talk, the making of threats or attempting to intimidate, or in any other conduct which causes a disturbance or a breach of the peace or threatened breach of peace. No person shall drive a motor vehicle onto the premises of a drive-in restaurant and leave the premises without parking such motor vehicle, unless there is no unoccupied parking space available on the premises. (d) It shall also be unlawful for any person to leave any unoccupied motor vehicle on any drive-in restaurant parking lot and leave the premises thereof except with the knowledge and consent of the operator of the restaurant. (e) It shall be the duty of each drive-in restaurant operator to post on the premises, in a conspicuous location, one (1) or more signs bearing the following legend: "Cruising in a motor vehicle is unlawful. Loud and offensive talk and other disturbance or breach of peace is prohibited. No unoccupied vehicle may be left on these premises without the consent of the restaurant operator."*

CALIFORNIA

Statewide:

- Due to a technicality in the California Vehicle Code, it can be illegal for a woman to drive while wearing a bathrobe.

- Looking out for the morals of school children, church goers, or drinkers, it is against the law for animals to publicly mate within 1,500 feet of a school, place of worship, or a tavern.

- A law was passed in a small town which outlawed anyone who tried to stop a child from playfully jumping over water puddles.

- It's unlawful in the state of California for either sex to fake an orgasm.

- The only things which can legally fall out of a vehicle are clear water or feathers from live chickens. *Actual Law: 23114. (a) Except as provided in Subpart I (commencing with Section 393.100) of Title 49 of the Code of Federal Regulations related to hay and straw, a vehicle shall not be driven or moved on any highway unless the vehicle is so constructed, covered, or loaded as to prevent any of its contents or load other than clear water or feathers from live birds from dropping, sifting, leaking, blowing, spilling, or otherwise escaping from the vehicle.*

- By policy, lizards and snakes are treated under the same guidelines in animal shelters as cats and dogs.

- Despite many claims to the contrary, it is legal to drive barefooted.

Apple Valley:

- Keep your quackers quiet (ducks that is) after 10:00 PM within the city limits.

Arcadia:

- When it comes to crossing a street or a driveway, a peacock has the right of way.

Bellflower:

- It is written somewhere that "a drunken man has as much right to a sidewalk as a sober man since he needs it a great deal more."

Belvedere:

- Actual Law: "No dog shall be in a public place without its master on a leash."

Berkeley:

- You cannot whistle for your lost canary before 7:00 A.M.

Beverly Hills:

- In this upscale community, it is written that "no male person shall make remarks to or concerning, or cough or whistle at, or do any other act to attract the attention of any woman upon or traveling along any of the sidewalks."

Blythe:

- You must have at least two cows before you are allowed to wear cowboy boots in this town.

Bonsal:

- A law once said that while church is in session, it is illegal to be on the front porch and read the Sunday paper while sitting in a rocking chair.

Buena Park:

- According to the morality police, males are prohibited from "turning and looking at a woman in that way" on Sundays. Getting caught twice carries the penalty of being required to wear horse blinders for a 24hour period in public."

Carmel:

- Until Clint Eastwood became mayor, it was illegal to eat ice cream while standing on a public sidewalk.

- Women may not wear high heels while in the city limits.

Castaic:

- As a bit of poetic justice, if your dentist accidentally pulls the wrong tooth, you can pull one of the dentist's teeth.

Cathedral City:

- After you park your vehicle, don't sleep in it.

- You cannot ride your bicycles in the "Fountain of Life".

Cerritos:

- You have only seven days to remove your dog's "droppings" from your yard.

Chico:

- It is illegal to own a green or smelly animal hide.

- Bowling on the sidewalk is against the law.

- Driving a herd of cattle down a street is against the law. *Actual Law: 9.44.020 Driving animals on streets prohibited. It shall be unlawful to drive, herd, or cause to be driven or herded upon any public street, alley, sidewalk or public place of the city any cattle, horses, mules, hogs, sheep or goats.*

- It is illegal to plant a garden on any public street.

- Detonating a nuclear device within the city limits could get you a $500 fine.

Compton:

- There is a rule which prohibits pants with hip pockets "since that is a good place to hide liquor."

Costa Mesa:

- Don't eat garlic less than four hours before going to a movie theatre.

Covina:

- A man cannot be convicted of desertion when his wife rents his room to someone else and "crowds him out of his house."

Dana Point:

- Exhibitionists beware, you cannot use your own bathroom if the window is open.

Downey:

- No matter how dirty it is, don't wash your car on a city street.

El Monte:

- Citing a limited number of places to sleep, it is reported that it is against the law for a horse to fall asleep in a bathtub unless the rider is also sleeping with the horse.

- Waitresses cannot drink with you. *Actual Law: It is illegal to buy your waitress a drink - Section 9.04.030 B-girls prohibited. No employee shall accept or solicit for himself or herself drinks of alcoholic beverages from any customer at the place where he or she is employed.*

Eureka:

- Playing ball with your child in the park can get you a ticket. *Actual Law: 93.55 BASEBALL PLAYING. It shall be unlawful to throw or hit or knock any baseball with a ball bat or any other instrument or engage in or play the game of baseball in any other manner on any city park or playground without first obtaining written permission to do so from the Director of Public Works. The Director of Public Works is hereby authorized and empowered to specify the conditions under which the game of baseball may be engaged in or played at any city park or playground. For the purposes of this section, the term 'baseball' shall mean any ball having a circumference of less than 11 inches or a weight of less than six ounces and which is commonly used in the game known as baseball.*

Fresno:

- No one may pester a horse, crow or a lizard in a city park, *Actual Law: SECTION 8-410. DISTURBING ANIMALS IN PARKS. No person shall hunt, pursue, annoy, throw stones or missiles at, or molest or disturb in any way, any animal, bird or reptile within the confines of any park.*

- There is no school for poker players & you cannot play poker within 300 feet of a school. *Actual Law: SECTION 8-121. GAMBLING ON OR ABOUT SCHOOL PROPERTY. No person shall play, participate in, or bet for or against any game not mentioned in Section 330 or 330a of the Penal Code of the State of California, in any public place or in any place exposed to the public view located within three hundred feet of any school if said game is played, conducted, dealt, or carried on with cards, dice, or other device, for money, checks, chips, credits, or any other thing which has or represents value.*

- Drunks cannot buy gas. *Actual Law: SECTION 8-124. SALE OF GASOLINE TO INTOXICATED PERSON. No person shall sell, loan, give or deliver gasoline to any person under the influence of intoxicating liquor.*

Gardena:

- A man can legally prevent his wife from chewing tobacco if he does not give her permission to do so.

Glendale:

• If you like horror movies, don't look for them between Thursday and Sunday. They can only be seen on Mondays, Tuesdays, and Wednesdays.

• Because of some serious problems related to their inappropriate use, you have to be 18 years old to buy a wax container. *Actual Law: 8.40.010 Findings - The council finds that: A. Large numbers of paraffin or wax containers are being discarded on the sidewalks of the city by children. Such containers, when discarded, become soft from the warmth of the sun and create a waxy, oily, greasy, slippery, dangerous and unsightly condition. The condition is aggravated because the contents of the containers attract large numbers of noxious flies. B. The discarded wax containers constitute a hazard to pedestrians and make the sidewalks unsafe for foot travel because of the greasy and slippery condition resulting on the sidewalks. Several persons have fallen because of that condition. Such containers are a hazard to the health of the city because of the number of flies attracted to them. C. Because of the hazard to pedestrians and the hazard to health and safety, the presence of the containers is a public nuisance. D. This public nuisance can best be abated by prohibiting the retail sale, gift or transfer of the containers to any person under the age of eighteen years in the city.*

• Keep that mutt out of the elevator. *Actual Law: 6.08.030 Restrictions Public elevators. No person owning or having charge, care, custody or control of any dog shall cause or allow it to go or be taken into any elevator in any office building, retail store or public building. This section shall not apply to dogs being used by the blind.*

Half-Moon Bay:

• We do not know who makes the definitions, but wearing a sweatshirt inside-out is defined as a "threatening misdemeanor."

Hermosa Beach:

- It seems like a no brainer, but public restrooms must be supplied with toilet paper.

- No matter how lovely they might be, no person can show his or her buttocks on a playground.

- It is illegal to pour salt on a highway.

Hesperia:

- Look out Aaron Burr: in this town "no one is allowed to duel if the opponent selects water pistols as weapons."

Hollywood:

- Two thousand sheep would be okay but driving two thousand and one sheep (or more) down Hollywood Boulevard is illegal.

Indian Wells:

- Having a grand opening? Do not use a trumpet player to draw a crowd into your store.

- Drinking intoxicating cement is prohibited.

- You cannot charge to tell fortunes or do it for donations either.

- Ex-cons will be glad to know that they cannot crush rocks within the city limits.

Inglewood:

- Winking can be a problem here. The law says it is illegal "for any male person, within the corporate limits of the city of Inglewood, to wink at any female person with whom he is unacquainted."

Lafayette:

- If you have to spit on the ground, make sure you are at least five feet from the closest person.

Lodi:

- Shooting "silly string" at people in a parade could get you a ticket.

Lompoc:

- It is illegal to have a rooster, regardless of the reason. They disturb the peace.

Long Beach:

- No matter how nice your tools are, the only thing allowed in your garage is your vehicle.

- Cursing while playing mini-golf is strictly prohibited.

- Dances have very specific dress codes for women, they: "must be found wearing a corset. A physician is required to inspect each female at the dance."

Los Angeles:

- It is against the law to bathe two babies in the same bathtub at the same time.

- It has been posted many times that "a man can legally beat his wife with a leather belt or strap, as long as the strap is no wider than 2 inches. The wife must give her consent in order for him to legally beat her with a wider strap."

- Keep your fingers to yourself at the butchers, because you will get a ticket if you poke a turkey to seek if it is tender enough.

- Moth hunting under a streetlight is prohibited.

- Don't even think about crying while testifying in court.

- Toads are to be watched, not licked.

- Because of some riots during World War Two, "Zoot suits" are prohibited in public.

Malibu:

- Laughing out loud in a movie theater could be considered disturbing the peace.

Monrovia:

- There are many ways to prove your manhood. In this town for a man to get married, he must- "prove his manhood" by shooting six blackbirds or three crows and bringing them to his prospective father-in-law."

Norco:

- This city has a bias against the oleander plant. *Actual Law: Section 6.08.010 Prohibition. No person, corporation or public agency shall plant or cultivate the oleander plant at any place in the city for any purpose whatsoever.*

- Vehicles may not contain sound systems which allow someone to hear noise outside the vehicle, unless you are trying to sell something.

- If you have some fireworks, keep them to yourself. You could get in trouble if you give them to someone else.

- You must get a permit to have a pet rhinoceros. *Actual Law: - Section 8.05.020 Permit--Definition. Except as provided in this chapter, no person shall possess, keep, maintain or have in his possession or under his control, within the city, any elephant, bear, hippopotamus, rhinoceros, lion, tiger, leopard, panther, ocelot, lynx, cougar, wolf, alligator, fox, raccoon, coyote, monkey, ape, chimpanzee, birds of prey, poisonous reptile, other dangerous or carnivorous wild animal, other vicious or dangerous domesticated animal or any other animal of wild or vicious propensities, without first applying to and receiving a permit from the city of Norco to do so.*

Ojai:

- A woman better bring a measuring tape with her when she goes out to a bar in Ojai. She cannot stand closer than five feet from a bar while drinking.

Ontario:

- You are in trouble if your rooster crows within the city limits.

Pacific Grove:

- Butterflies get special considerations in this town. It is illegal to pester or annoy them.

Palm Springs:

- Walking a camel down Palm Canyon Drive between 4 and 6 PM will get you a ticket.

Palo Alto:

- It is illegal to skateboard on walls "or other vertical surfaces".

Pasadena:

- Keep those office doors open, because a boss and a secretary cannot be alone in their office.

Pico River:

- Horseback riding by women wearing shorts and weighing over 200 pounds is prohibited.

Pomona:

- Having noisy teenagers can actually be against the law. *Actual Law:* "no person shall hallo, shout, bawl, scream, use profane language, dance, sing, whoop, quarrel, or make any unusual noise or sound in any house in such a manner as to disturb the peace and quiet of the neighborhood."

Portola:

- Be careful what you do on bridges in this city. *Actual Law: 9.36.010 Jumping or fishing from bridge or overpass—Prohibited. It shall be unlawful for any person to jump or fish from any bridge or overpass located within the city limits.*

Prunedale:

- It is illegal to have two indoor bathtubs in your house.

Redlands:

- This has to be a very old law. A man with a lantern must walk in front of any motorized vehicle using city streets.

Redwood City:

- Gravy cannot be fried in this town.

Rosemead:

- Use a spoon when you eat ice cream here, because using a fork will get you in trouble.

Riverside:

- Toting a lunch bucket down the street between 11 am and 1PM is illegal.

- Sticking your tongue out at a dog can get you a fine.

San Diego:

- You can do lots of things on a trolley here. Shooting jackrabbits from the back is not one of them.

- Christmas lights are considered a nuisance after February 2nd.

San Francisco:

- According to a local law "sunshine is guaranteed for the masses."

- If horse manure piles up on a street corner, it cannot legally be higher than six feet.

- Prostitutes do not legally have to make change for anything larger than a $50-dollar bill.

- No exotic animal (including giraffes) can walk down Market Street unless they are on a leash.

- If you are going to buff up the shine on your car, do not do it with used underwear.

- While we do not know who gets to determine this, you cannot walk down the street if you are considered "ugly."

San Jose:

- If you want to have pets, you are limited to a maximum of two dogs or cats.

Santa Ana:

- Swimming on dry land is prohibited.

- Letting your horse sleep in a bakery will cause trouble.

The Wacky World Of Laws: 2nd Edition

Santa Monica:

- According to old documents, "any person who shall in the city of Santa Monica use or carry a concealed or unconcealed any bean snapper or like article, shall, upon conviction, be fined."

- Playing drums on the beach can get you a ticket.

Shasta Lake:

- Raffling a dog is illegal. *Actual Law: 6.12.020 Selling, giving away or auctioning animals. It is a violation of this title to sell or give away unaltered dogs and cats in any public places or to auction off or raffle unaltered dogs and cats as prizes or gifts. No person in the city shall publish or advertise to city residents the availability of any unaltered cat or dog unless the publication or advertisement includes: the unaltered animal's license number, provided, however that nothing in this ordinance shall prohibit licensed breeders from advertising in national publications for sale of a planned litter or litter(s).*

Simi Valley:

- It's illegal to play baseball. *Actual Law: 10-1.03 Restricted acts. It shall be unlawful for any person within the limits of public schools, parks, recreation areas, and open spaces which are now or which may hereafter be within the City, including all grounds, roadways, avenues, parks, buildings, campgrounds, swimming pools, equestrian trails, bicycle trails, hiking trails, and school facilities under the control, management, or direction of either the Simi Valley Unified School District and the Simi Valley Recreation and Park District:(d) To play or engage in the flying of motorized or self-propelled model airplanes or rockets or motorized self-propelled model cars and boats, the driving of golf balls, archery, baseball, softball, football, soccer, volleyball, or any similar game of a hazardous nature, except at such places and times as shall be especially set apart for such purposes.*

Temecula:

- Ducks have the right of way to cross Rancho California Street at all times.

Thousand Oaks:

- You need a permit for a going out of business sale
Actual Law: Sec. 54.01. Permits: Required. It shall be unlawful for any person to advertise, represent, or hold out that any sale of goods, wares, or merchandise is an insurance, bankruptcy, liquidation, mortgage, insolvent's, assignee's, executor's, administrator's, receiver's, removal, or closing-out sale, or any particular department of such stock of goods, wares, or merchandise, under the guise of discontinuing business or discontinuing that particular department, or a sale of goods, wares, or merchandise damaged by fire, smoke, water, or otherwise, or a sale of goods from the stock of a bankrupt, receiver, trustee, insurance company, receivership, or trusteeship, or to conduct such sale unless he shall have first obtained a permit to conduct such sale from the City Manager.

Upland:

- Letting your animals "run at large" is against the law here. "

Ventura:

- It is illegal to make faces at dogs running around freely in the streets.

Victorville:

- Opening up canned peas by using a gun is strictly prohibited.

Whittier:

- An old law says: "two vehicles which are passing each other in opposite directions shall have the right of way."

Walnut:

- Men cannot dress like women. *Actual Law: 17-31 Male dressing as female. No man or boy shall dress as a girl or woman without a permit from the sheriff, except for the purpose of amusement, show or drama.*

- You have to have a permit from the Sheriff to wear a mask or a disguise. *Actual Law: 17-32 Mask or disguise— Wearing. No person shall wear a mask or disguise on a public street without a permit from the sheriff.*

- Kite flying is strictly limited to under 10 feet. *Actual Law: 17-1 Kite flying restricted. It shall be unlawful for any person to fly, above an altitude of ten feet above the ground, or near any electrical conductive public utility wires or facilities, any kite or balloon which has a body or any parts, tail, string or ribbon made of any metallic or electrical conductive material.*

- Putting sand on a driveway, including your own, is prohibited.

Wacky Case:

An author wrote a book about a man who was convicted of killing 16 people. The Orange County man was on death row in the California prison system. Claiming that "the characterization of him as a serial killer is false, misleading and defamed his good name," the prisoner sued the author for $60 million dollars. The convicted man claimed he was innocent of the 16 murders for which he had been found guilty. His lawsuit stated the book would make him "shunned by society and unable to find decent employment." That is, if he was ever release from death row and prison. It took the judge less than one minute to dismiss the case.

COLORADO

Statewide:

- Finally, a state has made it legal to rip off the tags on pillows and mattresses.

- One may not deface a rock in a state park.

- Showing cars on a Sunday is a no-no for car dealers.

- Don't even think about buying liquor on a Sunday or on Election day.

- It is illegal to ride a horse while under the influence of drugs and/or alcohol.

- People in Colorado are limited in their ability to catch rain in rain barrels. *Actual Law: Colorado Water Law requires that precipitation fall to the ground, run off and into the river of the watershed where it fell. Because rights to water are legally allocated in this state, an individual may not capture and use water to which he/she does not have a right. We must remember also that rain barrels don't help much in a drought because a drought by its very nature supplies little in the way of snow or rain. The reuse of household water (gray water) is regulated by the Colorado State Board of Health Guidelines on Individual Sewage Disposal Systems (PDF). Local health agencies are responsible for implementation and enforcement of the Guidelines.*

Alamosa:

- Throwing a missile at a car is dangerous and illegal.

- Keeping a house where unmarried persons are allowed to have sex is an offense.

- Persons may not urinate in public.

- You can own a new puppy without a license. Once it is over three months old, one must get a license.

Arvada:

- Establishments which sell alcohol must have enough lighting to allow you to read some text. *Actual Law: Sec. 3-4. Lighting. All licensees under this chapter shall be required to maintain a level of light within the licensed premises which would permit the checking of identification materials without resort to other lighting.*

Aspen:

- Snowball fights are against the law. *Actual Law: Section 15.04.210 Unlawful to throw stones, snowballs or discharge guns and other missiles. It shall be unlawful for any person to throw any stone, snowball or other missile, or discharge any bow, blowgun, slingshot, gun, catapult, or other device, upon or at any vehicle, building, or other public or private property, or upon or at any person, or in any public way or place which is public in nature.*

Boulder:

- Keep that rocking chair off of your porch. *Actual Law: 5-4-16 Outdoor Furniture Restriction. (a) No person shall place, use, keep, store, or maintain any upholstered furniture not manufactured for outdoor use, including, without limitation, upholstered chairs, upholstered couches, and mattresses, in any outside areas located in the following places: 1) In any front yard; (2) In any side yard; (3) In any rear yard or other yard that is adjacent to a public street. However, an alley shall not be considered a public street for the purpose of this subsection; or (4) On any covered or uncovered porch located in or adjacent to any of the yards described in paragraphs (1) through (3) above.*

• It is illegal to permit one's llama to graze on city property.

• You can insult a police officer only until they ask you to stop. Then it becomes illegal. *Actual Law: 5-3-6 Use of Fighting Words. No person shall insult, taunt, or challenge another in a manner likely to provoke a disorderly response. If the person to whom such insult, taunt, or challenge is directed is a police officer, there is no violation of this section until the police officer requests the person to cease and discontinue the conduct, but the person repeats or continues the conduct.*

Colorado Springs:

• Except for Sundays, Election Days, and or holidays, it is legal to strap on your six-guns.

Cripple Creek:

• It is illegal to bring your mule or horse above the first floor of any building.

Denver:

• Performing acrobatics which scare horses can get you a ticket.

• Rats have feelings, too. It is against the law to mistreat them.

• No matter how dirty their house gets, you cannot loan your vacuum cleaner to your neighbor.

- Before authorities can seize your dog, they have to give you notice (3 days).

- Driving a black car on a Sunday, that is not a hearse, is illegal.

Durango:

- Cross dressing is illegal if you do it in public.

Pueblo:

- Allowing a dandelion to grow within the city limits is prohibited.

Sterling:

- You could get in trouble if your pet cat runs free if they do not have a taillight attached to their rear end.

Wacky Case:

Vail, Colorado: 8-year old Scott Swimm was skiing at Vail, Colorado. Also on the slopes were David J. Pfahler and his wife. In December of 2007, Scott (then 7 years old) tried to pass Pfahler. He was skiing slightly uphill at under 10 mph. Pfahler suddenly turned into Swimm's path, and the two collided. Scott quickly, stood up, and apologized. As he turned to go, Pfahler reached over and grabbed Scott's ankle. Pfahler told Scott he was going to sue him for damages because of the collision. Pfahler said he suffered a torn tendon in his shoulder when he fell down. The Pfahler family sued for over $75,000 from Scott and his father (his legal guardian). The sum was to reimburse the Pfahlers for physical therapy expenses, lost vacation time and Mrs.

Pfahler's time "spent nursing her husband back to health." An out of court settlement was reached with the Pfahlers getting a $25,000 settlement.

CONNECTICUT

Statewide:

- According to state law, a pickle is not officially a pickle, unless it bounces when dropped.

- Lookout Lance Armstrong, bicycling over 65 miles per hour is illegal.

- It's illegal to keep town records in a liquor store. *Actual Law: Chapter 545 - Sec. 30-97. Town and probate records are not to be kept where liquor is sold. Town or probate records shall not be kept in any room in which alcoholic liquor is sold, nor in any room from which there is direct access to a room in which such liquor is sold. Any town clerk or judge of probate violating the provisions of this section shall be subject to the penalties provided in section 30-113.*

- An individual cannot dispose of their own used razor blades.

Devon:

- It is against the law to walk backwards after sunset.

Guilford:

- Only white Christmas lights are allowed for display.

Hartford:

- Do not educate your dog in Hartford.

- When you walk across the street, do not do it on your hands.

- Kissing your wife on a Sunday can get you into a legal jam.

Meriden:

- The use of a bean whistle in public is prohibited.

Rocky Hill:

- A total of four amusement games is all an arcade is allowed (Ex. pinball machines, ping-pong tables, or shuffleboard tables).

Southington:

- Similar to other cities, silly string is banned here.

Waterbury:

- It is illegal for any beautician to hum, whistle, or sing while working on a customer.

DELAWARE

Statewide:

- It is against the law to pawn a wooden leg.

- You cannot fly over any body of water unless you are carrying adequate amounts of food and drinks.

Fenwick Island:

- No Mobile homes are allowed in Fenwick Island. *Actual Law: 116-4. Activities inside vehicles prohibited. It shall be unlawful for any person to live, dwell, cook, sleep, change clothes or use toilet facilities inside any vehicle within the corporate limits of the Town of Fenwick Island, Delaware.*

- Movies with a rating higher than PG are not allowed to be shown at a drive-in theater. *Actual Law: - 1366. Outdoor motion picture theatres. (a) Whoever being the owner or operator of an outdoor motion picture theatre exhibits or permits to be exhibited any film not suitable for minors or harmful to minors and which film can be viewed by such minors not in attendance at the said outdoor motion picture theatre shall be guilty of a class A misdemeanor.*

Lewes:

- Getting married on a dare is grounds for an annulment.

- Wearing pants that are "firm fitting" around the waist is against the law.

Rehoboth Beach:

- Women cannot go topless. *Actual Law: 198-13. Topless bathing suits prohibited. No female over the age of **five years** shall wear a topless bathing suit or otherwise fail to cover her breasts with less than a full opaque covering of any portion thereof below the upper portion of the nipple.*

- Don't change your clothes. *Actual Law: 198-15. Changing clothes in comfort station prohibited. No person shall change his clothing from bathing suit to street clothes or otherwise within the comfort stations maintained by the city.*

- Whispering is illegal. *Actual Law: 198-23. Disturbing religious worship and lawful assemblies. A. No person shall disrupt or disturb any congregation or assembly met for religious worship by noise, talking or whispering, or by rude or indecent behavior, or by profane language within their place of worship, or within 300 feet of the place of worship.*

- Children can only trick or treat between 6 PM and 8 PM. *Actual Law: 198-33. Halloween regulations; exceptions. [Amended 10-14-1977 by Ord. No. 1077-2; 10-11-1991 by Ord. No. 1091-11 A. No person shall permit his child or any child under his control to go about the streets, ways and/or sidewalks within the corporate limits of the City of Rehoboth Beach for the purpose of causing mischief of any sort; provided, however, that children who have not attained the age of 14 years may go upon the streets, ways and/or sidewalks from door to door or house to house for treats between the hours of 6:00 p.m., prevailing time, and 8:00 p.m., prevailing time, on October 31 of any year; provided, however, that if October 31 shall be a Sunday, such going from door to door and house to house for treats shall take place on the evening of October 30 between the hours of 6:00 p.m., prevailing time, and 8:00 p.m., prevailing time.*

- Pretending to sleep on a bench on the boardwalk is not allowed.

- Alcohol may not be served in nightclubs where people are dancing.

DISTRICT OF COLUMBIA

- It is illegal for small boys to throw stones.

- A federal judge has ruled that begging is a form of free speech protected by the Constitution."

- Residents may not whistle in the bathroom.

- An establishment may not allow more than one accordion to be played for entertainment.

- One may not take photographs for more than five minutes in a public location.

- You cannot use a surfboard while on hallucinogens in the District of Columbia.

- Santa Clause cannot be used to sell alcohol.

- People cannot dance for more than 12 hours in a 24-hour period.

FLORIDA

Statewide:

•	It is illegal for a woman who is single, divorced, or widowed to parachute on Sunday.

•	It is against the law to fall asleep under a hair dryer. Both the hair dresser and the customer can get fined.

•	If you tie your elephant to a parking meter, you have to feed the meter just as if the elephant was a car.

•	It is illegal to sing in a public place while in a bathing suit.

•	Men wearing a strapless gown in public are violating the law.

•	Having sexual relations with a porcupine is not very wise, or legal.

•	Skateboarding can require a license.

•	The missionary position is the only legally approved sexual position.

•	You may not "pass gas" in a public place after 6 P.M. on Thursdays.

•	Under certain circumstances, a person may not "break more than three dishes per day, or chip the edges of more than four cups and/or saucers."

•	The penalty for horse theft was death by hanging.

The Wacky World Of Laws: 2nd Edition

- The Doors to all public buildings must open outwards. This came about in order for people to be able to evacuate a building quickly.

- It's illegal to have unmarried sex. *Actual Law: 798.02 Lewd and lascivious behavior. If any man and woman, not being married to each other, lewdly and lasciviously associate and cohabit together, or if any man or woman, married or unmarried, engages in open and gross lewdness and lascivious behavior, they shall be guilty of a misdemeanor of the second degree, punishable as provided in s. 775.082 or s.775.083.*

- The constitution says pregnant pigs cannot be confined while pregnant. *Actual Law: No. 10 Constitutional Amendment Article X, Section 19 Ballot Title: Animal Cruelty Amendment: Limiting Cruel and Inhumane Confinement of Pigs During Pregnancy Ballot Summary: Inhumane treatment of animals is a concern of Florida citizens; to prevent cruelty to animals as recommended by The Humane Society of the United States, no person shall confine a pig during pregnancy in a cage, crate, or other enclosure, or tether a pregnant pig, on a farm so that the pig is prevented from turning around freely, except for veterinary purposes and during the pre-birthing period; provides definitions, penalties, and an effective date.*

- In 2008, the Florida State Senate banned the display of fake testicles (called "Truck Nutz") on the back of vehicles. Often seen on large trucks and SUVs, owners said they added to the macho "truckliness" of the vehicle.

Big Pine Key:

- Molesting a Key deer could get you jail time.

Broward County:

- In this area folks need to be sure to stay appropriately attired when serving food from a food truck. *Actual Law: Chapter 39 ZONING* ARTICLE WII. COMMERCIAL DISTRICTS - Sec. 39-300. Limitations of uses. (s) Mobile food units. - (2) Persons vending from mobile food units who are inappropriately attired shall be considered to cause a hazard or impediment to traffic. Inappropriate attire shall include clothing which shows any portion of the anal cleft, cleavage or buttocks of males or females such as G-strings, T-back bathing suits, thong bikinis or any other clothing or covering that does not completely and opaquely cover the anal cleft, cleavage or buttocks of males and females. Inappropriate attire shall also include clothing which shows the portion of the human female breast directly or laterally below a point immediately above the top of the areola with less than a fully opaque covering. This definition shall include the entire lower portion of the human female breast, including the areola and nipple, but shall not include any portion of the cleavage of the human female breast exhibited by a dress, blouse, shirt, leotard, bathing suit or other clothing, provided the areola is not exposed.*

Cape Coral:

- It's illegal to hang your clothes in public.

- It is against the law to park a pick-up truck in a driveway or in front of a house on the street.

- Couches are not allowed in carports.

Daytona Beach:

- Don't work on your vehicle in your front yard.

- If your flowerpot cannot drain standing water, it can be considered a public nuisance. This is based on the mosquito problems related to Florida.

Destin:

- It's illegal to give away small birds. *Actual Law: Sec. 4-12. Sale or giveaway of certain animals. (a) It shall be unlawful for any person to sell, offer for sale, or give away in the city baby chickens, ducklings or other fowl under four (4) weeks of age, or rabbits under eight (8) weeks of age, to be used as pets, toys or retail premiums; or to give away or offer any animal as a prize, toy or merchandising premium.*

- Riding your bicycle in a cemetery can get you in trouble with the law. *Actual Law: Sec. 7-33. Traffic. (g) Bicycles prohibited. No person shall ride a bicycle on the grounds or property of any city cemetery.*

Hialeah:

- Walking very slowly can be illegal.

Key West:

- Do not race your turtles within the city limits.

Miami:

- Molesting an alligator will make the alligator and the authorities upset.

Miami Beach:

- No pigs are allowed inside city limits. *Actual Law: Sec. 10-7. Keeping swine within the city is prohibited. It shall be prohibited for any person to have in his possession, control, management or custody any swine within the city.*

- Any time a bicycle passes a pedestrian, it must make an "audible signal." *Actual Law: Sec. 70-69. Responsibilities of bicyclists and skaters. (c) Whenever any person is riding a bicycle, skateboarding, in-line skating, or roller skating, such person shall engage in such activity at a controlled speed which does not endanger the safety of pedestrians or others, shall yield the right-of-way to any pedestrian, and shall give an audible signal before overtaking and passing such pedestrian.*

Naples:

- According to "Sec. 106-34. General requirements:" Neon signs are prohibited in this town.

Palm Bay:

- It's illegal to pull anything behind you on your bike. *Actual Law: 72.45 TOWING - No operator of a bicycle shall tow or draw any coaster, sled, person on roller skates, wagon, toy vehicle or other similar vehicle on any public road, sidewalk or public place.*

Pensacola:

- Having less than $10 on you could be a violation of local vagrancy laws.

- Barrel rolling is illegal on most streets.

- Suicide by electrocution in a bathtub because of "self-beautification utensils" can cause legal problems for your estate.

Sanford:

- With the exception of a "bona fide" theatrical performance, nudity on stage is prohibited.

Satellite Beach:

- Naked Babies not allowed. *Actual Law: Sec. 38-61. Definitions. Nude means any person insufficiently clothed in any manner so that any of the following body parts are not entirely covered with a fully opaque covering: (1) The male or female genitals. (2) The male or female pubic area. (3) The female breast. (4) The buttocks. Body paint, body dyes, tattoos, liquid latex whether wet or dried, and similar substances shall not be considered opaque covering. Each female person may determine which one fourth of her breast surface area (see definition of breast) contiguous to and containing the nipple and the areola is to be covered.*

- Beer cannot be sold between 2 a.m. and 7 a.m.

Sarasota:

- You are not allowed to catch crabs in Sarasota.

Tampa Bay:

- Rats (and ship owners) can be punished for coming off of a docked ship.

- Topless dancing can only be performed if a woman's breasts are covered.

- While it is hardly a "lap dance", lap dances cannot be done within six feet of the customer.

Wacky Case:

In February 2004, Arlin Valdez-Castillo, a maid at the Hampton Inn at the Miami airport, filed a lawsuit claiming she got sick after cleaning up a room where five wild animals were kept. Busch Gardens was doing some publicity for their theme park in Tampa.

As a part of their campaign, Maya (spider monkey), Bob (alligator), Tango (Macaw) and Zuri and Rufio (lemurs), were kept in the room. Valdez-Castillo said that she made contact with "hair, feathers, urine and feces while cleaning the rooms and that the animal exposure left her with physical and emotional problems, including skin lesions throughout her body, headaches and depression."

Later in her testimony, she said two men kidnapped her, took her to a cemetery and threatened her if she did not drop the lawsuit.

Wacky Case:

Once in a Florida court, the opposing sides could not agree on anything. The judge tried to find numerous ways to arrange things which would suit both sides. After finding no acceptable solutions, the judge came up with a unique manner in which to proceed. To pick the location for a deposition, the judge ordered representatives from both parties to play a game of "rock, scissors, paper." The winner got to pick the location.

GEORGIA

Statewide:

- Advertising your prices is illegal for barbers.

- It is against the law to give your pet illegal drugs.

- It's illegal to give an elected state representative a speeding ticket. This is actually a law in many states. It was originally passed to keep law enforcement officers from keeping representatives away from important votes. In the "bad old days" some politicians would get a crooked cop to stop someone from getting to the capitol in time to vote against their lopsided legislation.

Acworth:

- Simply stated, all citizens must own a rake.

Athens-Clarke County:

- It's illegal to "pass gas" at the state fair. *Actual Law: Sec. 3-5-2. Disturbing meetings. No person shall create any disturbance at any public meeting or any place of amusement by loud talking, indecent or profane language, or any disturbing sound or action. (Ord. of 4-7-92, State law references: Preventing or disrupting lawful meetings, gatherings or processions.*

- If you are under 16, you had best get off the Xbox or PlayStation before 11 pm. *Actual Law: Sec. 3-8-3. Age and time restrictions. (a) Use of amusement machines by persons under the age of 16 years shall not be permitted during normal school hours on any day Clarke County schools are in session.*

(b) No person under the age of 16 years shall be allowed to operate any amusement machine after the hour of 11:00 p.m.

- A pig or a chicken running amok without a leash can get you in trouble. *Actual Law: Sec. 4-1-5. Livestock running at large. It shall be unlawful for the owner or keeper of any hog, cattle, mule, sheep, goat, fowl or any other livestock or nontraditional livestock animal to permit it to run at large in the limits of Athens-Clarke County or to stray from the property of the owner or keeper or to go upon the premises of any other person.*

- No 2fers when dealing with alcohol. *Actual Law: Sec. 6-3-7. Alcohol promotions. No licensee or employee or agent of a licensee shall engage in any of the following practices in connection with the sale or other disposition of alcoholic beverages: (1) The giving away of any ticket, token or any other item that can be exchanged for any alcoholic beverages with the sale of any other alcoholic beverage; (2) The sale of two (2) or more alcoholic beverages for a single price, or the sale of one (1) alcoholic beverage with a ticket, token or any other item redeemable for a subsequent alcoholic beverage. Also prohibited hereunder, is the sale of all such beverages a customer can or desires to drink at a single price.*

- Back rubs, massages and alcohol don't mix in this town. *Actual Law: Sec. 6-8-8. Alcoholic beverages. No person shall sell, give, dispense, provide or keep or cause to be sold, given, dispensed, provided or kept any alcoholic beverages on the premises of any massage business. (Ord. of 4-7-92, Ë] 12) Cross references: Alcoholic beverages. 6-3.*

Atlanta:

- Street lamps are not a legal place to tie up your pet giraffe.

- Piggyback rides are illegal if you are both males, because one man cannot be on another man's back.

Columbus:

- Skinny dipping is not allowed during the day. It does not seem to be prohibited at night. *Actual Law: Sec. 14-9. Bathing in public; suits required when. It shall be unlawful for anyone to bathe in any pond or branch within the corporate limits of the city between daylight and dark unless provided with suitable bathing suits, and no person shall bathe in the river anywhere between the north limits of the city and the southwest corner of the Exposition Park between daylight and dark, unless provided with suitable bathing suits; and from the southwest corner of park to southeast limit of the city persons may go in bathing at will.*

- Law enforcement must pay special attention to people who tease "idiots." *Actual Law: - Sec. 14-34. Idiots, etc.; teasing, harassing. It shall be unlawful and disorderly conduct for any person to tease or harass, either by words, signs or acts, on the streets or public places in the city any simple minded, idiotic, or crazy person, or any cripple, or other unfortunate person, and it is hereby made the special duty of the police department to enforce the terms of this section.*

- It's illegal to cuss. *Actual Law: Sec. 14-49. Profanity over telephone. It shall be unlawful for any person in the operation of any telephone installed within the city, to make use of any vulgar vituperation or profane language into and over such telephone.*

- Getting a tattoo is illegal on "Sundays and Sabbath days." *Actual Law: Sec. 14-60.3. Same Prohibited on Sunday or Sabbath days. It shall be unlawful for any person, individual or firm to conduct the business of tattooing or marking or coloring the skin by pricking in coloring matter so as to form marks or figures or scars on any portion of the body of any individual on Sunday or the Sabbath days.*

• If you have to remove a chicken's head, don't do it on Sundays.

• Nor, can you carry a chicken by its feet on a Sunday while walking down Broadway.

Conyers:

• Finding "slang talking" to be offensive, city leaders have prohibited saying the phrase "two fried eggs and a fritter for a quarter."

• It's illegal to leave a dead bird on your neighbor's lawn. *Actual Law: Sec. 11-3-7 Dead animals; disposition. No person shall place any dead animal upon his premises or upon the premises of any other person, or allow any dead animal to remain upon his premises or permit any dead animal belonging to the person to remain upon the premises of another without disposing of same or causing the animal to be properly removed or disposed of within 24 hours.*

Dublin:

• You must be kind to birds in this town. *Actual Law: Sec. 5-1. Molesting birds. The city is hereby declared a bird sanctuary and no person shall hunt, kill, trap or decoy birds or rob their nests of eggs or young in the city. It shall also be unlawful for any person to shoot at or shoot birds with a gun, pistol, "BB" gun, air rifle, slingshot, or other instrument of like kind, or strike, or throw any object at a bird.*

• Rat poison cannot be distributed without a license.

• Wearing a hood in Dublin can get you arrested.

- A game of catch in a city street could get you in trouble.

- Playgrounds are meant for people, so keep your car out of there.

Gainesville:

- They take their dining seriously in this town. They have a law which says chickens cannot be eaten with a fork.

Jonesboro:

- It is against the law to "oh boy" out loud in Jonesboro. Going back to post slavery days, a way to summon a freed man for some work was to yell "Oh boy." In bad economic times, this often led to a rush of out of work men. To avoid this mad rush, the expression was banned.

Marietta:

- You can spit from a truck, but not from a car or a bus.

Quitman:

- It doesn't matter if it has to get to the other side of the road, chickens cannot legally cross a street.

- Keep your autos off the sidewalks.

Roswell:

- Sunday is a day of rest for exotic dancers. *Actual Law: Section 4.2.1 Erotic dance establishment regulations. No licensee shall permit his place of business to be open on Sundays.*

HAWAII

Statewide:

- Keep your ears clear of pennies.

- Billboards are not allowed.

- A law once read that all citizens must own a boat.

- You may only have one alcoholic drink in front of you at a time.

- Men from the Orakama tribe may not eat their second wives.

- No child can be given the name "Charles".

- All girls under the age of 12 must own a grass skirt and take Hawaiian dance lessons.

- It is illegal to get a tattoo behind your ear or eyelid unless you are in the presence of a registered physician.

Honolulu:

- Birds are special. Unless you want to get in trouble, do not annoy them in a public park.

- Sunbathers cannot appear in their bathing suits in public on the streets of Waikiki.

- By law, twins must not work for the same company.

IDAHO

Statewide:

- According to an alleged state law, "it is illegal for a man to give his 'sweetheart' a box of candy weighing less than 50 pounds."

- Riding merry-go-rounds is not allowed on Sundays.

- Keeping track of beer is important here. Having an "unregistered, unlabeled beer keg is punishable by a maximum fine of $1,000 or prison for 6 months."

Boise:

- Fishing from a camel or giraffe's back is illegal.

Coeur d'Alene:

- Before a law enforcement officer can approach a vehicle where they suspect people are engaging in sex, the officer must honk their horn or flash their lights. Then the officer can approach after waiting for three minutes.

Eagle:

- While you can hide your dirt under your carpet, do not sweep it into the street. *Actual Law: 5-2-2: SWEEPING DEBRIS INTO STREETS: It shall be unlawful for any person to sweep any dirt, trash or rubbish from the interior of any building in the city onto any street, alley or sidewalk in the city.*

Idaho Falls:

- 88 is the maximum age for riding a motorcycle.

Pocatello:

- A concealed weapon is illegal unless someone can see it. *Actual Law• "the carrying of concealed weapons is forbidden, unless the same are exhibited to public view."*

- Don't get caught walking around in public without a smile on your face. Frowns are not appreciated.

Tamarack:

- Without a permit from the sheriff, you can only buy onions during the daytime.

ILLINOIS

Statewide:

- A state law requires that a man's female companion shall call him "master" while out on a date. The law does not apply to married couples.

- Animals can be sent to jail.

- Making faces at dogs is not allowed.

- You may not own a handgun.

Carbondale:

- Standing on the sidewalk in the 500 block of Illinois Avenue is not allowed.

- To prove you are not a vagrant, you must have at least $10 on you.

- Certainly an old law, before you can enter the city in an automobile, you must notify law enforcement.

Chicago:

- If a place is on fire, you cannot legally eat there.

- Do not give your dog alcohol.

- Even though it is known as the "Windy City," kites are not allowed.

- Do not spit in public. Period.

- Sitting on the curb and drinking beer out of a bucket will get you in trouble in the community of Pullman.

- If you want to protest naked outside of city hall, you must have a permit or be under 17 years old.

- A few years after the start of the 21st century, a law was passed which requires all contractors to post a notice stating if their company ever used slaves.

Cicero:

- Sunday is not the right day to go for a walk down a public street while humming.

Crete:

- Do not drive a car through town unless you are prepared to talk with the authorities.

Crystal Lake:

- Water usage and re-sodding your lawn has certain restrictions. You cannot water new sod with city water. If you water it with non-city water, you must have a permit.

Decatur:

- It is illegal to drive a vehicle which does not have a steering wheel.

Des Plaines:

- If you want to sell your wheelbarrow, do not tie it to a tree with a For Sale sign.

Eureka:

- Men with mustaches cannot kiss women in public.

Evanston:

- No bowling is allowed.

- If you need to change your clothes while in an automobile without curtains, there better be a fire. Otherwise, it is illegal.

Freeport:

- Don't spit out of any window above the first floor.

Galesburg:

- A smelly bird could get you in trouble. *Actual Law: Sec. 4-6. Noise, odor, etc. No person shall keep or maintain any animal, poultry or fowl in such a manner to cause inconvenience or disturbance to other persons by reason of noise, odor or other cause.*

- Abusing a rat, with a baseball bat, could get you a fine.

- Do not burn feathers.

- Be polite in crowds, because "jostling" is not allowed.

- If you must demonstrate some "fancy riding" on your bicycle, make sure you are not on a city street.

Horner:

- Only cops are allowed to use a slingshot.

Joliet:

- Looking for some new clothes? After trying on six dresses in one store, you must move on.

- Mispronouncing this town's name could get you a fine. "Joe-lee-ette" is the only legal way to say it. Saying it as "Jolly-ette" is just not done.

Kenilworth:

- If your rooster must crow, you better be at least 300 feet from any other resident.

Kirkland:

- Simply stated, the city of Kirkland prohibits bees in its skies or in its streets.

Moline:

- Ice skating at the Riverside pond is not allowed from June to August.

Morton Grove:

- If you want to shoot something, you best have a shotgun. Anything smaller is illegal.

Oblong:

- We will not comment on this posting. It should speak for itself. "it is illegal to make love while hunting or fishing on your wedding day."

Park Ridge:

- Trucks cannot park on city streets.

Peoria:

- Do not put up a basketball hoop over your driveway.

Winnetka:

- While you might get away with talking in a movie theater, anyone with "odiferous feet" can be removed by the manager.

Zion:

- No matter how cute the photos might look, dogs, cats, and other domesticated animals are not allowed to be given lit cigars.

Wacky Case:

In this case, an Alton attorney accidentally sued himself. In 2005, Attorney Emert Wyss took on the case of a woman who thought she had been overcharged in a real estate deal. Wyss agreed to represent her against the alleged company. The only problem was, Wyss owned the company in question. According to reports, before the incident was over, he had hired four other firms to handle various parts of the claim against himself.

INDIANA

Statewide:

- According to state law, you no longer have any rights to your breath once it leaves your lips.

- Bathing during winter months (October to March) can cause problems for you if someone wants to enforce a very old law.

- All hotel bed sheets must measure 99 inches long by 81 inches wide.

- Fishing with a crossbow could get you a ticket.

- Places that sell alcohol cannot offer any "inducements" such as discounted prices.

- "Tail lights" are not allowed on pedestrians.

- Parking spaces are only to be used with the front end of the vehicle going in first. No backing in.

- Minors in a vehicle must wear shoes.

- Who knows why, but swallowing a match is illegal.

- Puppet shows must be free.

- You are not failing to support your children if you only pray for them when they get sick. *Actual Law: IC 35-46-1-5 Sec. 5.(a) A person who knowingly or intentionally fails to provide support to the person's dependent child commits nonsupport of a child, a Class D felony. However, the offense is a Class C felony if the amount of unpaid support that is due and* *owing is at least ten thousand dollars ($10,000). (b) It is a defense that the child had abandoned the home of his family without the consent of his parent or-on the order of a court, but it is not a defense that the child had abandoned the home of his family if the cause of the child's leaving was the fault of his parent. (c) It is a defense that the accused person, in the legitimate practice of his religious belief, provided treatment by spiritual means through prayer, in lieu of medical care, to his dependent child. (d) It is a defense that the accused person was unable to provide support.*

- Visiting a hypnotist requires a note from a licensed physician, unless it is to quit smoking or lose weight.

- In another old law, passing a horse on a street with an automobile is illegal.

- It is posted that liquor stores cannot sell cold soft drinks.

- Patrons in restaurants cannot legally carry their own drink from the bar to their table. A server must do it.

- Gossipers beware, it is illegal to "talk behind a person's back" or to engage in "Spiteful Gossip."

- Back when the infrastructure was being created, all men between the ages of 18 and 50 had to work six days a year on the public roads.

- Playing cards can get you a fine.

- Pi should equal the whole number of 3, not 3.1415. In 1897, Bill Number 246 was introduced into the Indiana General Assembly. It passed the House and was postponed indefinitely in the Senate. It still remains on hold, as far as we know.

Auburn:

- Don't ride anything self-powered on wheels in a commercial zone. It will get you a fine.

Beech Grove:

- Watermelons are not allowed in city parks. Other small melons are legal.

Elkhart:

- Barbers are not allowed to threaten to cut off a young person's ears if they will not hold still.

Evansville:

- Keep your lights off while driving on Main Street.

Fort Wayne:

- The recording "It's In the Book" is not allowed to be sold or played on the air in this town.

Gary:

- Eating garlic less than four hours before riding on public transportation or being in a public place is illegal.

- Donkeys are not allowed inside city limits.

Indianapolis:

- Junk or rag collecting is not allowed on Sundays and Holidays. *Actual Law: Sec. 401-103. Rag and paper collecting. No person shall engage in the occupation of paper or rag collecting or general junking on foot, or by handcart, automobile or other vehicle, before the hour of 7:30 a.m. or after the hour of 5:30 p.m., except in the area of the city bounded on the north by North Street, on the south by South Street, on the east by East Street, and on the west by West Street; provided, however, no paper or rag collecting shall be permitted at any time of the day or night on Sundays or legal holidays. Actual Law: Sec. 441-105. Effect of this chapter on horses and other animals. No horse or other animal, either driven or ridden, shall be left unattended, unhitched or insecurely fastened upon any street or public place, or hitched or left at any place when and where the parking of motor vehicles is prohibited and, when so left, the horse or other animal and any vehicle drawn by it shall be subject to all applicable provisions regulating motor vehicles at any such time and place. No horse shall be driven or ridden on any street in the city at a speed in excess of ten (10) miles per hour and every horse shall be kept under control at all times by the person in charge thereof. Such person shall be subject to all applicable traffic regulations that apply to motor vehicles.*

South Bend:

- Monkeys cannot smoke cigarettes.

Warsaw:

- Throwing "hard things" across the street is illegal. *Actual Law: Sec. 54-61. Throwing objects across streets, alleys, sidewalks and other public places. It shall be unlawful for any person to throw any snowball, stone or other hard substance, or any other missile along, across or over any street, alley, sidewalk or other public place within the limits of the city.*

IOWA

Statewide:

- Kisses may last up to five minutes.

- Ministers, Priests, and Rabbis cannot take wine across state lines. *Actual Law: Chapter 221 Wines for Sacraments, etc. Section 1. Wines for sacraments, etc. purchase and transportation - permit. Any minister, priest, rabbi, of any church, sect, denomination or creed which uses wines in its sacrificial ceremonies or sacraments, and who desires to purchase and have transported by either intrastate or interstate common carriers and have possession of such sacramental wines shall, before purchasing or transporting such sacramental wines apply for and obtain a permit authorizing such sale or transportation as hereinafter provided. Approved April 14, 1919.*

- Stores featuring tanning beds must warn users that there is a risk of them getting sunburned.

- Men with mustaches cannot kiss women in public.

- Unless a piano player has two arms, they must perform for free.

Bettendorf:

- Beer ads cannot be posted outside liquor stores.

Cedar Rapids:

- No form of fortune telling is allowed. *Actual Law: 62.25 FORTUNE TELLING. No person shall tell fortunes or practice phrenology, palmistry or clairvoyance in the city.*

Dubuque:

- A law going back to the old days still requires that all hotels have a hitching post and water buckets.

Fort Madison:

- Before going to a fire, the fire department must practice fire fighting for fifteen minutes. It is believed this law was misprinted.

Indianola:

- Ice cream trucks are not allowed here.

Marshalltown:

- They might look tasty, but horses should not eat fire hydrants.

Mount Vernon:

- If you are playing softball, you will be playing it in the dark. *Actual Law: 47.06 SOFTBALL DIAMOND LIGHTS. The lights at the Mount Vernon softball diamond shall be used only for organized games and tournaments unless permission is obtained from the Parks and Recreation Director. In no event, shall the lights at the ballpark be on after 10:30 p.m. on any night.*

- Do not pick the flowers in a city park.

- If you want to throw (or place) bricks on the highway, you must first obtain a permit.

Ottumwa:

- A man cannot wink at a woman he does not know in this town.

KANSAS

Statewide:

- It is illegal to catch fish with your bare hands.

- Do not shoot at rabbits from a boat.

- You cannot hunt ducks while on another animal's back.

Cranium County:

- The words "monkey" or "ape" cannot be used too closely to the word "human" during a speech near or at a school.

Derby:

- Animal-drawn vehicles are prohibited. *Actual Law: 10.12.050 Riding animals and animal-drawn vehicles. A. It is unlawful for any person to ride or allow or permit any other person to ride upon any horse or other animal, or drive or operate any animal-drawn vehicle, on any street, roadway, highway, or public ground in the city at any time other than while participating in a scheduled parade or public display. The chief of police may give prior written consent for a designated person to ride or allow a horse or other animal upon a designated boulevard, road, street, or drive, or upon public ground as defined in this section, during certain designated hours and under supervision of the police department. B. Every person riding an animal or driving or operating any animal-drawn vehicle upon a street, roadway, or highway shall comply in all respects with the Standard Traffic Ordinance as adopted by the city. C. As used in this chapter, public ground is defined as any land owned by the city or any land which has been dedicated for the sole and exclusive use of the city. Public ground does not include public utilities and easements. D. Any person who violates any provision of this section is guilty of a misdemeanor and shall upon conviction be punished by a fine not to exceed one hundred dollars.*

- You cannot hit a vending machine which did not give you the item you purchased from it.

- Tire squealing is prohibited.

- Marriage and skateboards do not mix according to the law.

Dodge City:

- All business must have a trough of water for horses.

Lawrence:

- Having bees in your bonnet is not allowed.

- Honk your horn before you drive your car into the town.

McLough:

- Washing your false teeth in a public water fountain is both improper and illegal.

Natoma:

- This notice was found: 'it is against the law to practice knife throwing at men in striped suits."

Overland Park:

- You cannot picket a funeral. *Actual Law: 11.28.064 Funeral Picketing 1. Definitions a. As used in this section, funeral means the ceremonies, processions and memorial services held in connection with the burial or cremation of the dead, as well as memorial services held in connection with the death of any person. b. As used in this section, picketing means protest activities engaged in by a person or persons stationed before or about a cemetery, mortuary, church, mosque, synagogue, temple, or other place for religious observances, or other places for funeral services, during the period from 60 minutes before to 60 minutes after any funeral. 2. It is unlawful for any person to engage in picketing during the period from 60 minutes before to 60 minutes after any funeral at any cemetery, mortuary, church, mosque, synagogue, temple, or other place for religious observances, or other places for funeral services. 3. Each day on which a violation of this section occurs shall constitute a separate offense. (History: Ord. POC1792ffl 1, 93)*

Russell:

- Musical car horns are prohibited.

Topeka:

- Watch what you haul across the road in this town. *Actual Law: Sec. 545. Hauling on Kansas Avenue restricted. No stable manure, offal, house refuse, garbage, night soil or dead animals shall be hauled along Kansas Avenue except over the Kansas Avenue Memorial Bridge.*

- You had better not annoy anyone with your late-night serenade in this town. *Actual Law: Sec. 54-158. Yelling, shouting, etc. Yelling, shouting, hooting, whistling or singing on the public streets, particularly between the hours of 11:00 p.m. and 7:00 a.m., or at any time or place so as to annoy or disturb the quiet, comfort or repose of persons in any office, or in any dwelling, hotel or other type of residence, or of any persons in the vicinity, is unlawful.*

- Wine cannot be served in teacups in public houses.

Wichita:

- Bean snappers are prohibited.

KENTUCKY

Statewide:

- A woman cannot be on a highway in a bathing suit. *Actual Law: no female shall appear in a bathing suit on any highway unless she is escorted by at least two officers of the law or unless she be armed with a club". An amendment to the law says that "the provisions of this statute shall not apply to females weighing less than 90 pounds nor to females exceeding 200 pounds, nor shall it apply to female horses." bathing suit on any highway within this state. section 1376m-1, 1376m- 2. Repealed: January 1, 1975.*

- Dyed baby animals must only be sold in groups of six. *Actual Law: - KRS 436.600 - No person shall sell, exchange, offer to sell or exchange, display, or possess living baby chicks, ducklings, or other fowl or rabbits which have been dyed or colored; nor dye or color any baby chicks, ducklings, or other fowl or rabbits; nor sell, exchange, offer to sell or exchange or to give away baby chicks, ducklings or other fowl or rabbits, under two (2) months of age in any quantity less than six (6), except that any rabbit weighing three (3) pounds or more may be sold at an age of six (6) weeks. Any person who violates this section shall be fined not less than $100 nor more than $500. History: Amended 1972 Ky. Acts ch 374, sec 1. —Created 1966 Ky. Acts ch. 215, sec. 5.*

- Throwing a shoe at a public speaker could get you a hefty fine. *Actual Law: - KRS 437.050 Attempting to interrupt or injure public speaker Any person who interferes with any person addressing a public audience within this state, who interrupts such a person, while speaking, by the use of insulting or offensive language or opprobrious epithets applied to the speaker or who attempts to interrupt or injure the speaker by throwing missiles of any kind at him shall be fined not less than fifty ($50.00) nor more than five hundred dollars ($500), or* *imprisoned for not less than one (1) year nor more than six (6) months [sic], or both.*

- It is illegal to fish with a bow and arrow.

- It's illegal to fish in Kentucky on the Ohio River without an Indiana Fishing License.

Fort Thomas:

- Dogs are not allowed to annoy cars.

Lexington:

- No ice cream cones in your pocket, please.

North Quiverburgh:

- Use of an image showing a human naval, nostril, toe (or other body part) in a school requires approval by religious authorities or the constable.

Owensboro:

- A woman must get her husband's permission before buying a hat.

LOUISIANA

Statewide:

- You are allowed to grow as tall as you would like.

- If you rob a bank and then shoot a teller with a water pistol, you could get in even more trouble.

- Biting someone with your original teeth is classified as "simple assault". Biting someone with your false teeth is classified as "aggravated assault."

- Do not steal alligators. *Actual Law: - RS 14:67.13 67.13. Theft of an alligator - A. Theft of an alligator is the misappropriation or taking of an alligator, an alligator's skin, or a part of an alligator, whether dead or alive, belonging to another, either without the consent of the other to the misappropriation or taking, or by means of fraudulent conduct, practices, or representations. An intent to deprive the other permanently of the alligator, the alligator's skin, or a part of an alligator is essential.*

- Do not steal crawfish. *Actual Law: RS 14:67.5 67.5. Theft of crawfish; penalty - A. No person shall knowingly, willfully and intentionally fish or take any commercial crawfish from any crawfish farm, except with the consent of the owner thereof.*

- Do not mock the Boxers at a fight. *Actual Law: - RS 4:8181. Open betting or quoting of odds; insulting or abusive remarks - - There shall be no insulting or abusive remarks made by seconds, managers, or spectators and directed at the contestants. The officers of the club, and the secretary of the commission, shall at once eject persons who violate this or any other provision of this chapter.*

- Fake Wrestling is prohibited. *Actual Law: RS 4:75 75. Sham or fake contests or exhibitions - Whoever conducts or is a party to any sham or fake boxing contest or wrestling exhibition shall forfeit his license and shall not thereafter be entitled to receive any license pursuant to the provisions of this chapter.*

- Daring someone to trespass on someone else's railroad tracks could get you a ticket.

- Despite religious freedom, any rituals which involve swallowing blood, fecal matter or urine are not allowed.

- Promising something you do not plan on doing can get you jail time.

- If you get a serious burn, you must report it to the fire marshal.

- Hurting yourself in prison can get you a longer term.

- It is rude and illegal to gargle in public places.

Jefferson Parish:

- Minors cannot play coin-operated foosball games in a public place without an adult with them.

- Pouring out a drink at a drive-in movie is messy and illegal.

- Your garbage must be cooked before you feed it to your hog. *Actual Law: - Sec. 7-187. Preparation of garbage, etc., fed to hogs. - All garbage, refuse, offal or other material other than grain foodstuffs to hogs must be cooked on the premises just prior to the feeding of the hogs.*

New Orleans:

- Fortune telling is prohibited. *Actual Law: - Sec. 54-312. Fortunetelling. It shall be unlawful for any person to advertise for or engage in, for a moneyed consideration, the business of (chronology, phrenology, astrology, palmistry), telling or pretending to tell fortunes, either with cards, hands, water, letters or other devices or methods, or to hold out inducements, either through the press or otherwise, or to set forth his power to settle lovers quarrels, to bring together the separated, to locate buried or hidden treasures, jewels, wills, bonds or other valuables, to remove evil influences, to give luck, to effect marriages, to heal sickness, to reveal secrets, to foretell the results of lawsuits, business transactions, investments of whatsoever nature, wills, deeds and/or mortgages, to locate lost or absent friends or relatives, to reveal, remove and avoid domestic troubles or to bring together the bitterest enemies converting them into staunchest friends. But nothing herein contained shall apply to any branch of medical science, or to any religious worship.*

- Alligators should not be tied to a fire hydrant.

- Long ago, a law said that a man must wave a flag in front of his wife if she was driving a car.

Port Allen:

- Fortune telling is prohibited.

- Picketing has certain restrictions. Picketers must be at least five feet apart. Only two people may be on a sidewalk at a time.

Sulphur:

- No phone sex. *Actual Law: Sec. 8-136. Telephone communications, improper language, harassment - (a) No person shall: (1) Engage in or institute a telephone call, telephone conversation, or telephone conference, with another person, anonymously or otherwise, and therein use obscene, profane, vulgar, lewd, lascivious, or indecent language, or make any suggestion or proposal of an obscene nature or threaten any illegal or immoral act with the intent to coerce, intimidate, or harass another person.*

- Alcoholism is illegal.

- It is legal in some places, but no drive-thru liquor stores are allowed here.

MAINE

Statewide:

- It is illegal for anyone to step out of a perfectly good airplane while it is in flight (no skydiving allowed).

- Long ago, all male citizens had to carry shotguns when they went to church in case of an attack by American Indians. The law did not say what American Indians should do in case they were attacked.

- Dog leashes may not be over 8 feet long.

Augusta:

- Playing a violin while strolling down the street in this town is prohibited.

Biddeford:

- Gambling at the airport is not allowed.

- You cannot roller skate on the sidewalks.

Ellsworth:

- Local laws take precedent over federal ones.

Portland:

- Tickling a girl under her chin with a feather duster might look cute, but it is against the law.

- You cannot walk down the street if your shoelaces are untied.

Rumford:

- Biting your landlord is strictly prohibited.

South Berwick:

- Parking in front of the Dunkin Donuts is not allowed.

Waterville:

- Please do not blow your nose in public.

Wells:

- Feeding deer can get you a ticket. *Actual Law: 80-17. Prohibited conduct; exceptions. - No person, except the Commissioner of the Maine Department of Inland Fisheries and Wildlife or his/her designee or the Director of the United States Fish and Wildlife Service or his/her designee, shall feed or bait deer in the Town of Wells. This prohibition shall not apply within the boundaries of the Rachel Carson National Wildlife Refuge, which is property owned by the United States and managed by the United States Fish and Wildlife Service.*

- Cemeteries are not allowed to post commercial advertisements.

MARYLAND

Statewide:

- Lions are not allowed to attend the theatre.

- Condoms may only be dispensed by vending machines "in places where alcoholic beverages are sold for consumption on the premises".

- You cannot keep your chickens with you in your hotel room.

- It is illegal to play professional croquette before 2pm on Sundays.

- It is necessary to record any services performed by a jackass.

Baltimore:

- Throwing a bale of hay from a second story window can get you a trip to the courthouse.

- Within a week of Easter, minors cannot legally buy chicks, chickens, ducks, ducklings or roosters.

- No one is allowed to have a Thistle on their lawn.

- Shirts without sleeves are prohibited in public parks.

- Spitting on city sidewalks is bad. Spitting on the road is OK.

- Cursing is not allowed in public areas.

- You are not allowed to pester, bother, annoy or mistreat an oyster.

- In some circumstances, scrubbing your sink could get you into trouble.

Columbia:

- Cursing in public is not allowed here, either.

- Satellite dishes are allowed, but visible antennas are illegal.

- You may dry your clothes on your fence, but not on a clothesline.

Halethrope:

- Long kisses (defined as longer than five seconds) are illegal in public.

Ocean City:

- Men must wear shirts while on the boardwalk.

- Eating while you are swimming in the ocean is not just bad for you here, it is illegal.

Wacky Case:

In this case, a certified masseuse wanted to be able to massage horses. Mercedes Clemens says the state of Maryland would not let her massage horses because she was not a veterinarian. Clemens loved horses and she wanted to show them the same care she could legally give to humans. She sued two state agencies to get their rulings changed. Before the state put a halt to her business, she had 30 regular equine customers.

MASSACHUSETTS

Statewide:

- Tomatoes are not allowed in clam chowder.

- Diapers cannot be delivered on Sundays.

- There is a maximum number of sandwiches you can eat at a wake. That number is three.

- If your feet are hot, do not hang them out a window to cool them off.

- Judges do not like it if you eat peanuts in court.

- The only people who can shoot at human silhouettes at a firing range are law enforcement officers while performing official duties.

- Taxi drivers are not supposed to make love in their taxis during working hours.

- Displays of public affection are often prohibited in front of places of worship and on religious holidays.

- It was once the law that Sunday was the only day livestock could not graze on public held land.

- Rodeo Clowns are not supposed to make love in front of the horses since it might spook them.

- Atheism or blaspheme can get you in real trouble.
Actual Law: PART IV. CRIMES, PUNISHMENTS AND PROCEEDINGS IN CRIMINAL CASES TITLE 1. CRIMES AND PUNISHMENTS - CHAPTER 272. CRIMES AGAINST

CHASTITY, MORALITY, DECENCY AND GOOD ORDER - Chapter 272: Section 36. Blasphemy - Section 36. Whoever willfully blasphemes the holy name of God by denying, cursing or contumeliously reproaching God, his creation, government or final judging of the world, or by cursing or contumeliously reproaching Jesus Christ or the Holy Ghost, or by cursing or contumeliously reproaching or exposing to contempt and ridicule, the holy word of God contained in the holy scriptures shall be punished by imprisonment in jail for not more than one year or by a fine of not more than three hundred dollars, and may also be bound to good behavior.

- Long ago, you needed a special permit to wear a goatee.

- Snoring so loudly that others can hear it is illegal.

- Only so much alcohol is allowed in candy. *Actual Law: Chapter 270: Section 8. Selling candy containing alcohol. - Section 8. Whoever sells to a person any candy enclosing or containing liquid or syrup having more than one per cent of alcohol shall be punished by a fine of not more than one hundred dollars.*

- The "missionary position" is the only legal position.

- Back seats of cars are not a good place to put your gorilla.

- Tattooing and body piercing were once illegal.

- Once upon a time being a Quaker or a witch was illegal.

- Bullets may not be used as money.

- Massachusetts liquor stores can only open on Sundays if they are in certain counties: "Berkshire, Essex, Franklin, Middlesex or Worcester counties and are within 10 miles of the Vermont or New Hampshire borders."

Boston:

- Frog jumping contests are not allowed.

- Baths were once limited to twice a month.

- Playing the fiddle is severely limited by law.

- Two people may not kiss in front of a church.

- At one time, duels were only allowed if the Governor was a witness.

- High heels were once illegal for women walking on the commons.

Cambridge:

- Permits for Gaelic football, hurling, and soccer cost more than other events.

Fitchburg:

- Barbers cannot carry their combs in their hair or head.

Hingham:

- Any house visible from Main Street can only have white lights outside their house.

- The historical society must approve any changes or painting done to your house.

Holyoke:

- Residents are required to turn off sprinklers when it is raining.

Hopkinton:

- Dogs cannot play in the commons, even though cows and horses can graze there.

Longmeadow:

- If you must carry your bathtub across the commons, you are required to have three or more men do it.

Marlboro:

- Squirt guns are strictly prohibited.

- Silly string is not legal either.

Milford:

- Looking into the windows of a car can get you a ticket.

Nahant:

- Do not slide down a street on your sled.

Newton:

- Every new family moving to town is supposed to receive a free pig from the mayor.

North Andover:

- "Space guns" are not allowed here.

Woburn:

- Once your beer is served, you cannot walk around with it.

MICHIGAN

Statewide:

- Dogs can be killed for attacking people or livestock. However, they cannot be killed by decompression chamber or by electrocution.

- If either a husband or wife kisses their spouse on a Sunday, they have broken an old law.

- At one point, a law was passed which paid a bounty for the head of each rat which was brought into a city hall.

- Owning a handgun (and the appropriate license) is legal for anyone over twelve years old who has not been convicted of a felony.

- Another old law says a woman must get her husband's permission before cutting her hair.

- At one time, cursing in front of women and children was illegal. This law has been revoked, assumedly because women and children now curse, too.

Clawson:

- Sleeping with your livestock can get you in trouble. *Actual law: "it is legal for a farmer to sleep with his pigs, cows, horses, goats, and chickens."*

Detroit:

- Destroying old radios is illegal.

• Showing anger toward your spouse on a Sunday is prohibited.

• A pig on the loose in Detroit better have a ring in their nose. It makes them easier to catch, and keeps them from rooting for things to eat.

• Because throwing things onto the ice can hamper a hockey game, Joe Louis Arena authorities can seize anything "throwable." Having a throwable octopus (which became a fad at one point), can get you a ticket.

• Sex in a vehicle is only legal when the vehicle is parked on your property, and you are not visible to your neighbors.

Grand Haven:

• Disposing of a hoop skirt on a street or sidewalk is littering and a violation of the law.

Harper Woods:

• Painting a sparrow to make it look like a parakeet for the purpose of commerce is a legal no-no.

Kalamazoo:

• Serenading someone can get you in trouble with music critics and law enforcement.

Rochester:

• Police officers have the authority to inspect the bathing attire of anyone wearing it in public.

Wayland:

- Grazing your cattle on Main Street is legal, if you purchase a permit.

MINNESOTA

Statewide:

- Mosquitoes are officially a public nuisance.

- Loitering is still illegal here.

- Who knows why, but if you have a duck on your head, you cannot legally cross the state line into this state.

- Sleeping in the nude could garner some legal troubles if you are discovered.

- Topless motorcycle riding (shirts, that is) is prohibited for men. Women are prohibited from being topless in public by other laws.

- Your bathtub must have feet.

Blue Earth:

- Perhaps to avoid crank calls, no one under twelve years old can use a phone without adult supervision.

Cottage Grove:

- You can only water your lawn on certain days. Even numbered addresses can do it on even numbered days. Odd numbered residents get odd numbered days.

Hibbing:

- Law enforcement must kill all cats running free. *Actual Law: It shall be the duty of any policeman or any other officer to enforce the provisions of this Section, and if any cat is found running at large, or which is found in any street, alley or public place, it shall be the duty of any policeman or other officer of the city to kill such cat.*

Minneapolis:

• Driving down Lake Street in a red car is disrespecting local ordinances.

Minnetonka:

• Talking anyone into visiting a massage parlor is illegal.

• Having sex with your masseuse has restrictions. You cannot marry them for two years after.

• Trucks with extra dirty tires can be breaking the law.

• Putting tacks on a sidewalk is not considered funny or legal.

St. Cloud:

• Hamburger eating on Sundays violated local rules.

Winona:

• A public nuisance is defined as any cottonwood tree which "sheds its seeds profusely."

• Annoying, bothering, killing, molesting or trapping squirrels is a not allowed.

- Livestock is not allowed to mate within public view within city limits.

<u>Wacky Case:</u>

It is illegal for a massage therapist to marry a former customer for at least two years after their last professional encounter. The archaic law also states that they cannot engage in sex, even if they are married after the two-year waiting period.

A contestation of this law took place in Lindstrom, Minnesota. An antagonized ex-wife reported to authorities that her ex-husband had married his former massage therapist. The ex-wife wanted the therapist to lose her license to practice and be charged with a crime. The ex-wife was sure the married couple was engaging in intimate encounters with each other, despite the legal prohibition. Talk about rubbing someone the wrong way!

MISSISSIPPI

Statewide:

- A citizen's arrest for anyone disturbing a church service is legally justifiable.

- Teaching anything about polygamy was once outlawed.

- Saying you will marry someone in order to engage in sexual activity is strictly forbidden.

- Profanity in public places is positively prohibited.

- You can still be hanged for rustling cattle.

- Horses must be kept at least 50 feet from any road.

- Cohabitating, as well as natural or unnatural sexual activity with another unmarried person, are both illegal.

- Being sexually aroused in public is more than just impolite here.

- A man can go to jail for fathering two or more illegitimate children.

- Only wrestlers are allowed to accept a bribe on order to fix a match or a game.

Canton:

- Killing a small furry animal in a courtroom with a handgun is illegal.

Columbus:

- You can get in more trouble by waving a gun around than you can for actually shooting it (assuming you don't hit anyone).

Hazelhurst:

- Moving fish down a street is difficult and may be illegal.

Meridian:

- Rolling a safe down the road under its own power, or pushing its own wheels, can get you a fine.

Oxford:

- Circumnavigating the town square is strictly limited based on the number of times you do it in a row.

- Do not honk your horn if it might scare a horse.

Ridgeland:

- If you add exterior burglar bars to your house, make sure they blend into the architecture.

Roswell:

- Smooth, non-absorbent floors are a legal requirement for stores selling "adult entertainment materials."

Tylertown:

- Follicle removal cannot be done on Main Street.

MISSOURI

Statewide:

- Although it sounds like a bogus law, any town wishing to raise taxes to support an official band, must meet this requirement: "the mayor plays piccolo and each band member can eat peas with a knife."

- Whenever you move a bear down a highway, it must be in a cage.

- In the early 1800s, a law was passed that taxes each single man, between 21 and 50 years old, $1 a year.

Buckner:

- Do not burn your yard clippings on a Sunday.

Clandestine:

- Being homesick for Monrovia on Palm Sunday is not grounds for singing about your longings for the old country.

Excelsior Springs:

- No one can throw anything hard.

- Annoying, bothering, pestering, or worrying a squirrel will get you a written reprimand.

Kansas City:

- Youngsters cannot purchase cap guns. They can purchase a shotgun, if they have a note from an adult.

- Bathtubs can have "feet" as long as the feet do not look like animals.

Marceline:

- A child can buy their grandparent tobacco and rolling papers, but not a lighter.

- Four women who are not related cannot live alone in the same residence. This was once the definition of a brothel.

Merryville:

- Corsets are prohibited on women. *Actual Law: the privilege of admiring the curvaceous, unencumbered body of a young woman should not be denied to the normal, red-blooded American male.*

Mole:

- Scaring a child, and making them cry, is not only a bad thing to do, but you can get a ticket for it.

Natchez:

- Alcoholic beverages shall not be given to animals, domestic or wild.

Purdy:

- Dancing is not allowed in this town.

St. Louis:

- Drinking beer from a bucket is severely limited here. It seems there is an old custom imported from Italy which involves drinking beer from a bucket.

- Running with full milk bottles is not a good idea. It can be illegal for the milk man.

University City:

- Polyvinyl Chloride pipes (PVC) were banned.

- If you have a yard sale, it cannot be held in public view (not in your yard). If you have a sale out of public view, you are limited to two events a year.

- Bright lights which bother your neighbors are not allowed.

- Honking your horn is not allowed. *Actual Law: 10.32.100 Climbing into another's vehicle, sounding horn, etc. prohibited without permission. No person shall, without the permission of the owner or person in charge thereof, climb upon or into, or swing upon any motor vehicle or trailer, whether the same is in motion or at rest, or sound the horn or other sound producing device thereon, or attempt to manipulate any of the levers, starting device, brakes, or machinery thereof, or set the machinery in motion.*

MONTANA

Statewide:

- Never sacrifice an animal when a youngster can see you do it. *Actual Law: - 45-5-627. Ritual abuse of minor — exceptions — penalty. (1) A person commits the offense of ritual abuse of a minor if the person purposely or knowingly and as part of any ceremony, rite, or ritual or of any training or practice for any ceremony, rite, or ritual: (b) actually or by simulation tortures, mutilates, or sacrifices an animal or person in the presence of the minor.*

- A woman cannot open her husband's mail without his written permission.

- At one time, movies depicting a felony act were banned.

- While it has been revoked, it was once legal to consider the gathering of seven or more Indians as a hostile act. It was legal to attack them, even if they had not threatened anyone.

Billings:

- Rats can only have two legal uses: food for other wild animals, or for use in scientific research.

- Wandering minstrels are not allowed in any place which serves alcohol. *Actual Law: - Sec. 3-301. Live entertainment to remain on platform while performing. - The owner or proprietor of an establishment selling alcoholic beverages for on-premises consumption may permit in the establishment instrumental and/or vocal music or entertainment and/or radio and television entertainment whether such entertainment is provided by paid or voluntary live male or female entertainers or performers or by mechanical, electrical, electronic or other comparable device or equipment; provided, that all live entertainment as herein specified shall be performed on a platform or other exclusive area provided for such purpose, and no entertainer or performer whether male or female shall be permitted to leave such platform or area while entertaining or performing.*

- "Pea shooters" are not allowed.

- Speed-dialing is severely limited in this town.

Helena:

- Do not toss things across a street.

- Do not turn your sprinklers on to get passersby wet. *Actual Law: 5-9-2: Lawn Sprinklers - No person shall place any revolving fountain, hose or lawn sprinkler so that the water from the same shall be thrown upon any street or sidewalk to the annoyance of passersby, and no person shall cause water to flow over or upon any street or sidewalk.*

- While it is surprising they allow it at all, folfing is only allowed during the day, unless you are on an officially sanctioned folfing course. "Folfing" is another name for Frisbee golf. *Actual Law: - 5-13-2: Folfing Prohibited - No person shall play or engage in the game of folf or throw a folf disc at nighttime in any area within the business improvement district that has not been sanctioned as a designated folf course by the city.*

- For a woman to be allowed to dance on a table, she must be wearing at least three pounds, two ounces of clothing.

Kalispell:

- Pool tables are only allowed in a billiard hall if they can be seen from the nearest road. *Actual Law: 19-30 Screens in Pool Rooms - It shall be unlawful for any person or the agent of employee of any person owning or conducting any place of business wherein is kept any pool table, billiard table or bagatelle table to place in front of the room or across the inside of the room, wherein is kept any such pool table, billiard table or bagatelle table for hire or gain, any screen, blind, curtain, shutter, painted, colored or ground glass or any article of furniture or any obstruction that would prohibit the view of such pool table, billiard table or bagatelle table from the street in front of such room or place of business wherein is kept any of the tables above described.*

Sheridan:

- Animals which might defile a fire hydrant (mainly dogs), cannot get any closer to this firefighting tool than four feet.

Whitehall:

- Studded tires can only be used on icy roads. Please do not try to use ice picks or the ends of forks as studs.

NEBRASKA

Statewide:

- Children causing disturbances during a church service can get their parents in legal troubles. No burping, please.

- In order to allegedly protect the law-abiding and healthy community, it is illegal to marry anyone who has a sexually transmitted disease (STD). *Actual Law: - 42-102 - Minimum age; affliction with venereal disease, disqualification. At the time of the marriage the male must be of the age of seventeen years or upward, and the female of the age of seventeen years or upward. No person who is afflicted with a venereal disease shall marry in this state.*

Hastings:

- Sleeping in the nude in a hotel is frowned upon in this town. Hotel managers are supposed to offer each guest a clean nightshirt to avoid violating this law.

Lehigh:

- Doughnuts = legal. Doughnut holes = illegal.

Waterloo:

- Barbers can only eat onions, or other foul-smelling foods, during certain hours.

Wacky Case:

Assuming being shot five times was not enough of a problem, authorities also kept one man's wooden leg. Val McCabe was shot five times in Nebraska. In order to access one of the bullets lodged in his wooden leg, authorities confiscated it. The police maintained they needed the leg in order to test the bullet which landed there.

The District Attorney argued that authorities needed extended access to the leg in order to perform a battery of tests on it. McCabe convinced a judge that his specially built artificial leg (costing $28,000 when he got it) could not be easily replaced by any alternative means. After police removed the bullet, the leg was returned by a court order.

NEVADA

Statewide:

- Bar owners must boil soup and sell beer - To make it legal for bar owners to sell beer, they must be simultaneously boil up some soup.

- It is illegal to conceal a spray-painted shopping cart in your basement.

- Sex without a condom is considered illegal in some places.

- You can bet on any sports team except the University of Nevada at Las Vegas.

- A man caught beating his wife can be tied to a stake for eight hours with a sign that tells the world he is a "wife beater".

Clark County:

- Concealed handguns are allowed if they are properly registered with local law enforcement. The weapon can only be brought in for the required inspection on a weekday.

Las Vegas:

- You can pawn almost anything to pay for your gambling, except your false teeth.

Nyala:

- Sharing can get you in trouble. There are limits on how many people you can buy drinks for.

Pahrump:

- Prostitution is legal, but for a while, speaking any language in this town other than English was not.

Reno:

- You can walk, skip or stroll down the sidewalks. Just do not sit down on one. *Actual Law: - Sec. 8.12.015. Sitting or lying down on public sidewalks in the downtown redevelopment district prohibited. - (b) Except as otherwise provided in this section, no person shall sit or lie down upon a public sidewalk, or upon a blanket, chair, stool, or any other object placed upon a public sidewalk in the downtown redevelopment district, as it is defined in section 18.07.040 of the Reno Municipal Code.*

NEW HAMPSHIRE

Statewide:

• You literally cannot sell the shirt off your back to pay a gambling debt.

• Keeping time to the music, with any external part of your body, in any public establishment which serves food or drinks is not permitted.

• Do not use a nom de plume to register at a hotel or motel.

• Certain livestock cannot cross a state road unless they are wearing a special thing which collects their "droppings."

• Sunday is not the day to operate certain machines.

White Mountain National Forest:

• Be careful what you do here, even if you are trying to help. You cannot rake leaves, sweep the beach, remove trash, fix a structure, or many other things without a permit. If you do, you could be fined for "maintaining the national forest without a permit.'

NEW JERSEY

Statewide:

- Keeping a homing pigeon from returning to their home is illegal.

- Horse carriages always have the right of way.

- Getting a DUI/DWI conviction can cause you to lose your personalized license plates.

- Wearing a bulletproof vest, while committing a crime, is prohibited. *Actual Law: - 2C:39-13. Unlawful use of body vests - 1. Unlawful use of body vests. A person is guilty of a crime if he uses or wears a body vest while engaged in the commission of, or an attempt to commit, or flight after committing or attempting to commit murder, manslaughter, robbery, sexual assault, burglary, kidnapping, criminal escape or assault under N.J.S.2C:12-1b. Use or wearing a body vest while engaged in the commission of, or an attempt to commit, or flight after committing or attempting to commit a crime of the first degree is a crime of the second degree. Otherwise it is a crime of the third degree. As used in this section, "body vest" means bullet-resistant body armor which is intended to provide ballistic and trauma protection.*

- Some people who live here say you cannot legally knit at a fishing hole during fishing season.

- Do not make faces at law enforcement personnel.

- Pumping your own gas is not allowed.

- People who slurp their soup are considered nuisances.

- Young people cannot legally purchase functioning handcuffs.

- Who knows why you would want to do this but raising chickens in a bottle is illegal.

Barker:

- Ringing doorbells or knocking on doors could be considered disturbing the peace.

Bernards Township:

- This township is a "Frown-Free Town Zone". So, keep that frown upside-down.

Blairstown:

- Trees which block the light and air are prohibited. *Actual Law: 171-2. Shade trees. The streets of the township shall be used for the purpose of public travel only, with such other use of the same as is necessarily connected with public travel. Shade trees may be planted along the streets, highways, and alleys, but not within the prescribed limits of the same. Such trees shall be planted so as not to obscure light and air and shall not be so close as to interfere with the lawful use of such streets, highways and alleys. They shall be properly trimmed by the owners of adjoining premises. No person shall wantonly or negligently cut or destroy any such shade trees without the consent of the owner of the adjoining premises and of the Committee and occupants.*

- Marine crafts are not supposed to be parked in front of your house.

Caldwell:

- Do not dance on the main street here while wearing shorts.

Cresskill:

- Cats which go outside must wear bells to warn nearby birds.

Elizabeth:

- A woman walking on Brad Street on a weekend must wear a petticoat or an underskirt.

- Do not bother people of the opposite gender.

- Do not wear clothes which are intended for the opposite gender.

- Do not remove the labels from your bathing suit regardless of gender.

Liberty Corner:

- Honking your horn, while making whoopee in your car, could be considered a crime.

Manville:

- Do not give, or offer to give, alcohol or tobacco to animals at the zoo.

Mount Laurel:

- Annoying anyone while you are under the influence is illegal even on private property. It is illegal to get drunk and annoy others in your house.

Newark:

- Buying certain foods after 6pm (such as ice cream) is illegal unless you have a note from your doctor.

Ocean City:
- Slurping your soup could be considered disturbing the peace.

- Playing pinball on a Sunday is not legal.

- Selling uncooked hamburgers is not allowed at a restaurant.

Raritan:

- Cursing in public is not allowed.

Sea Isle City:

- Making soup aside, boiling bones, even in your own home, is against the law.

Trenton:

- Sunday is not the day to eat or buy pickles.

- It is considered littering if you dispose of a bad pickle in the street.

Wacky Case:

In Camden County, a woman complained that during spinal surgery while she was anesthetized, someone affixed a temporary tattoo of a red rose on her stomach. She complained this was done without her permission or knowledge. She did not discover the tattoo until the next morning while she was getting dressed to leave. The rose was placed below her panty line.

Her surgeon stated he often left temporary tattoos on his patients in order to lift their spirits. He denied that the location of the tattoo had any sexual connotations. According to the surgeon, none of his previous patients had complained.

Because her surgery was on her back, the woman said the tattoo had to have been added after the surgery. She said she would have been lying on her stomach during the procedure. She wondered what real purpose could have been served by rolling her over and then applying a tattoo in this location. She filed an official complaint with the New Jersey Board of Medical Examiners.

NEW MEXICO

Statewide:

• Authorities considered Shakespeare's "Romeo And Juliet" too steamy because it contains "sexually explicit material." To make it more appropriate for public morals, they deleted approximately 400 words from the classic play.

• Gambling on bicycle races is illegal but camel and ostrich racing are okay.

• It is illegal for cab drivers to reach out and pull passengers into their vehicles.

• The state constitution prevents "Idiots" from voting.

Carrizozo:

• Women cannot appear in public if any part of their visible skin needs to be shaved.

Las Cruces:

• Carrying a suspicious lunchbox down Main Street could cause you legal problems.

White Horse:

• An old law once said that in order for a married woman to eat onions on a Sunday, her husband had to be armed and nearby.

NEW YORK

Statewide:

- Arresting a dead man is not allowed.

- Unwanted and overt flirting can leave with a citation.

- Urinating on wild animals is bad manners and almost always illegal.

- Under certain circumstances, women can be topless in public. However, those circumstances do not extend to "purposes of business."

- Not watching where you are going could make you a nuisance. So be careful while eating chestnuts and walking backwards.

Albany:

- Golf is not allowed on city streets.

Brooklyn:

- Parents have been advised to properly instruct their children in the use of the area's local slang and Jargon. The proper use of the word "Yo" is an example of the subject matter.

Carmel:

- A man wearing a mismatched shirt and pants is subject to tickets and fines.

- Eating messy foods like ice cream at a bus stop can get you a ticket.

New York City:

- All store window mannequins must be dressed.

- According to an often-published note, "it is legal for a woman to ride the subway topless since it is legal for a man to ride the subway topless."

- Do not clean your dust mop by shaking it outside of a window.

- Throwing a ball at someone's head for fun is not only rude, it is illegal.

- Hanging clothes on a clothesline requires a license.

- Being found guilty of attempted suicide which places others at risk is punishable by death. This is why jumping off a building could kill you either way.

- Slippers are not proper footwear on city streets at certain times of the day.

- It is obvious that this law is seldom enforced, but at one time women wearing "body hugging clothing" could be given a summons.

Ocean City:

- Eating, while swimming, is not suggested or allowed.

- Men with large breasts might be required to wear an appropriate shirt.

- Eating in the middle of a street in a neighborhood is not safe or legal.

- The only legal beverage on the beach is water in a clear, non-glass container.

Sag Harbor:

- Do not change your clothes while in a moving vehicle.

- All "bathing" must be done while wearing appropriate bathing attire.

Wacky Case:

A 25-year old man from Queens sued Amtrak after he was electrocuted and burned while riding on their train. This happened in 2006 after he broke into the out-of-service train so he could get a free ride when the train returned to service, At the time of the incident, the man was intoxicated from a night of partying. As he stood on the top of the train, he touched the 27,500 volt overhead lines.

The man had third degree burns on 85% per cent of his body. Parts of his left hand and leg were amputated. His defense in the lawsuit was that Amtrak should have known that people would try to break into their trains in order to steal a ride. His lawyer said that Amtrak should have taken the appropriate steps to prevent people from breaking into their trains. They should have also turned off the electricity when the trains were not running. They should have known that people would trespass on their property and their trains.

NORTH CAROLINA

Statewide:

- Plowing cotton fields, and almost all forms of animal powered labor, is not allowed with wild animals. So, keep that elephant in the zoo.

- Singing out of tune could be considered a public offense.

- According to an old law, if you register at a boarding house as a married couple for immoral purposes, you might actually be considered married for real.

- Anyone in possession of illegal drugs must pay taxes on them. They are still illegal, but you have to pay taxes on them too.

- Wearing a disguise can be illegal. This is why many groups cannot hold a meeting if their members are in costumes.

- Fortune telling is illegal, unless you are doing it for free at a church or a school.

- The "missionary position" is the only legal position. Your curtains must be pulled shut while in that position.

- Suffering from erectile disfunction can be grounds for voiding a marriage.

- Only blind people can use white canes in public.

Asheville:

- Do not sneeze in this town.

Barber:

- Dogs and cats are not legally allowed to fight here.

Chapel Hill:

- Horses cannot be ridden at high speeds or on sidewalks.

Charlotte:

- Women in skimpy clothes are violating the law which says they must wear, at least, 16 yards of clothing.

Dunn:

- Cars must stay out of cemeteries unless they are there for the appropriate purposes.
- Late night visits to a cemetery are illegal, too.

Forest City:

- An old law, which may still be on the books, says you must warn public officials before you drive an automobile into this town.

Greensboro:

- Outdoor menus must not be so large as to be legible from the street.

Kill Devil Hills:

- Both hands must be on your bike's handlebars whenever it is in motion.

Rocky Mount:

- A dog is considered property in this town. As such, you must pay property tax on it.

Southern Shores:

- State highways are not the place to try out your roller skates.

Topsail Beach:

- Legally, hurricanes cannot enter this beach town.

Wade Mills:

- Buying food too close to the start of church services might violate the laws here.

Winston-Salem:

- College students must be at least seven years old.

Zebulon:

- Stay off this town's water towers. *Actual Law: 130.05 CLIMBING ON ROOFS AND WATER TANKS. - (A) It shall be unlawful for any person to climb or tramp on any of the roofs of any business houses in the Town without a lawful purpose. - (B) It shall be unlawful for any person to climb or go on the ladder or any part of any water tank owned by the Town without the permission of the Town Manager or the Chief of Police.*

• Lurking outside a police station after dark might get you a ticket.

NORTH DAKOTA

Statewide:

• Beer and Pretzels may not be served at the same time in a bar or restaurant.

• Sleeping with your shoes on could violate some social customs and laws.

Devil's Lake:

• Fireworks may not be set off after 11 pm. This includes on New Year's Eve.

Fargo:

• Dancing and hat wearing do not mix in this town. So, do not do both at the same time.

OHIO

Statewide:

- Because of certain "modesty issues" women are required to not wear patent leather shoes in public.

- Seducing female students by skating instructions is specifically prohibited.

- Playing outdoor games such as croquet or horseshoes too close to official "Decoration Day" activities could get you a ticket.

- A certain edition of the Ohio driver's education manual says passing another car requires honking your horn.

- Public breast feeding can be illegal.

- Not showing due respect to things of "great importance" can cause problems.

- Leaving your keys in your ignition is illegal because it can contribute to car theft.

Bay Village:

- Escorting livestock down Lake Road is not allowed.

Bexley:

- According to "Ordinance #223," Slot machines are not allowed in out buildings such as outhouses.

Canton:

- Losing your exotic pet requires prompt notification of the legal authorities.

- "Power Wheels" are not legal on public roads.

- Games played in the public park must be approved by the park superintendent.

Cleveland:

- Sitting on someone's lap is not the proper place to be when driving a vehicle.

- Catching any kind of wild animal, such as a mouse, requires a license.

Clinton County:

- Leaning on a public building could be considered loitering, and would therefore be illegal.

Columbus:

- Many kinds of things cannot be sold here on Sundays.

Fairview Park:

- Excessive horn honking is illegal. Determining what is excessive is up to the court.

Ironton:

- Men may not wear women's garments in public except in a socially acceptable manner as part of an organized theater production.

Lima:

- No map of Ohio can be sold in this town if the town does not appear on the map.

Lowell:

- Horses cannot go faster than five miles per hour here.

MacDonald:

- Walking a barnyard animal down Main Street is not allowed

Oxford:

- Women may not remove their clothing in a provocative manner while standing in front of a man's picture.

Paulding:

- If absolutely necessary, a law enforcement official can bite a dog.

Toledo:

- Reptile throwing is considered too scary to be legal.

Youngstown:

- Running out of gas on the local roads is illegal.

- The roof of a taxicab is not the proper place to sit.

The Wacky World Of Laws: 2nd Edition

OKLAHOMA

Statewide:

- Eating other people's food is not nice or legal.

- Feeding alcohol to your fish, or other wild animals, is illegal.

- At one time, authorities required women to have a license before they could cut anyone's hair, including their own.

- Reading a comic book, or any other kind of book, is illegal while driving.

- Making faces at a dog could annoy the dog and public officials.

- Tattoos are not allowed.

- Wearing boots to bed has been shown to be illegal in certain circumstances.

- Unmarried people may not engage in intimate activities.

- Pretending to have sex with a buffalo once got someone in trouble with the law.

Ada:

- Supporting the New York Jets football team by wearing their uniforms could put you in legal jeopardy.

Bartlesville:

- There is a legal limit to the number of cats you may own if you are not a cat breeder.

- Causing annoying vibrations has been banned here.

- Baseball is not allowed in city streets.

Clinton:

- Putting things into an automobile that could cause damage is not allowed.

Cushing:

- One must be properly attired in order to drink beer in public. Wearing only underwear is not considered appropriate attire.

Duncan:

- Clothes must not be washed in inappropriate places, such as a birdbath.

Hawthorne:

- According to city Ordinance #363, hypnotized people may not be displayed in a public window.

Schulter:

- If a woman wants to gamble she must wear proper clothing. Being nude, wearing lingerie or seductive clothing is not proper.

Shawnee:

- Keeping more than three dogs requires a permit, even if they are not yours.

Tulsa:

- Special bottles may only be opened under the supervision of an appropriate engineer.

- Wild animals are not allowed in downtown unless they are properly restrained.

Wynona:

- Bird baths are not considered to be an appropriate watering hole for livestock.

Yukon:

- When riding your horse downtown, do not tie it up in front of city hall.

- Horn honking is appropriate when you pass another vehicle.

OREGON

Statewide:

• Removing your socks is required to enter the Pacific Ocean, according to a court decision.

• Until recently, pumping your own gas was illegal.

• Babies are supposed to ride inside of automobiles, not on the running boards. *Actual Law: 811.205 Carrying child on external part of vehicle; penalty. (1) A person commits the offense of carrying a child on an external part of a motor vehicle if the person carries any child upon the hood, fender, running board or other external part of any motor vehicle that is upon a highway. (2) The offense described in this section, carrying a child on an external part of a motor vehicle, is a Class B traffic violation.*

• Human waste should be placed in jars on the side of the road. *Actual Law: 811.172 Improperly disposing of human waste; penalty. (1) A person commits the offense of improperly disposing of human waste if the person is operating or riding in a motor vehicle and the person throws, puts or otherwise leaves a container of urine or other human waste on or beside the highway. (2) The offense described in this section, improperly disposing of human waste, is a misdemeanor and is punishable by a maximum fine of $250.]*

• A certain law related to medicine (called the "Peer Review Statute") means the only thing you can learn about your medical treatment is what the medical personnel want to tell you.

• "Talking dirty" is not even allowed while engaged in intimate activities.

- Having clothing which covers you from the neck to the knees is still part of an old bathing suit law.

- It is not considered correct to use canned corn as fishing bait.

Corvallis:

- Drinking coffee after 6pm is not permitted for females.

Eugene:

- Sundays are not the correct days to arrange to see a movie or be involved in a race.

Hood River:

- Juggling is strictly regulated by law.

Klamath Falls:

- Because of the way the sidewalks used to be built, and the habit of rattlesnakes to pop their heads up between the slats, kicking the heads off of snakes was prohibited.

Marion:

- Not watching where you are going and being distracted could make walking backwards while eating a doughnut illegal.

- People giving speeches in public should refrain from eating garlic, onions or other foul smelling foods.

Monmouth:

- An unescorted woman may not enter the car of a man she does not know, unless it is an on-duty taxi.

Myrtle Creek:

- Boxing with a kangaroo is not allowed.

Portland:

- Skating rinks are not the proper place to have a wedding ceremony.

- Your shoelaces should always be tied properly.

- "Offensive physical contact" is just not tolerated.

Salem:

- Wrestling is not acceptable for women.

Springfield:

- The only place a reptile can be legally kept is in a school or a zoo.

Stanfield:

- You cannot have cloth towel machines in public bathrooms.

- Multiple people sharing one drink is not permitted.

Willowdale:

- "Talking dirty" is not allowed even among consenting and married partners.

PENNSYLVANIA

Statewide:

- Sixteen unmarried women living in the same house (other than a sorority) meets the definition of a brothel.

- Singing in the bathtub can be prohibited if it bothers anyone.

- A law was once posted which made it illegal to sweep household dirt under a rug.

- Whenever the bride or groom is drunk, a wedding ceremony cannot be performed.

- Weddings are festive. However, shooting off a gun or a cannon is considered too much.

- This is probably "case law," but sleeping outside on top of a refrigerator is not permitted.

- An old law once required motorists to stop every mile, send up a flare, and then wait ten minutes for the livestock to have a chance to get out of the way.

- Another old law required a motorist to pullover whenever they spotted an oncoming horse team. After pulling over, they had to cover their vehicle with a blanket which would make it blend in with the countryside. All of this was to keep the horses from getting spooked.

- Citizens of Pennsylvania are not allowed to purchase fireworks within the state.

- You cannot buy more than two boxes of beer at a regular store.

- The state must operate all official liquor stores.

- Using a hook on a line is okay for catching fish. Using just your hands is not.

- Do not go fishing with dynamite.

- Participating in a duel will eliminate you from a future as Governor of the state.

- A hunting club says you need a license to hunt on your own property. This is not true for fishing on your own property.

- Before a man can buy alcohol, he must get his wife's permission.

Allentown:

- No outward evidence of a man "being in the mood" is acceptable.

Bensalem:

- Bingo is highly regulated in this town. No advertising of game prizes allowed.

- Felons cannot run a bingo parlor.

Connellsville:

- Pants which sag more than five inches below your waist are not allowed.

Danville:

- A fire hydrant can only be used for a fire if it passed a checkup at least an hour before.

Morrisville:

- The "natural look" is preferred here. Women are not allowed to wear cosmetics unless they have a license to do so.

Newton:

- Before you can legally install an electrical switch or power outlet, you must purchase a permit and have it inspected.

Pittsburgh:

- Livestock are not allowed on local trolleys.

Tarentum:

- Parking meters are not to be used as a hitching post.

RHODE ISLAND

Statewide:

- At one time, it was prohibited to use words like dwarf, midget, runt, shrimp, small, teenie-weenie, teensy-weensy, or tiny when discussing Rhode Island, or its government.

- It is illegal to pretend to be an auctioneer, town sealer, fence viewer, or a cord of wood. *Actual Law: TITLE 11 - Criminal Offenses CHAPTER 1114 False Personation SECTION 11-14-2 -- 11-14-2 Impersonation of town sealer, auctioneer, corder, or fence-viewer. Every person who shall falsely assume or pretend to be a town sealer of weights and measures, auctioneer, corder of wood, or fence-viewer, and shall act as such, shall be fined not less than twenty dollars ($20.00) nor more than one hundred dollars ($100).*

- Cap guns are strictly prohibited. *Actual Law: Title 11 Criminal Offenses Chapter 11-13 Explosives and Fireworks Section 11-13-4: Toy canes or devices for firing blanks. No person or persons shall sell, expose for sale, possess with intent to sell or use, or discharge or use, within this state, any repeating toy cane for discharging any explosive, any toy pistol, or any other toy device designed or used for the discharge of blank cartridges.*

- Before passing a vehicle on the left, honking your horn is mandated.

- Horseracing on public highways is illegal.

- Forcing anyone under your supervision to do anything they do not wish to do on Sundays is prohibited.

- Most organized sporting events held on Sunday are required to get a license.

- The exception is hockey and ice polo.

- Being an idiot or lunatic (acceptable legal terms) will prohibit you from getting married.

- Throwing vegetables, such as a pickle, at trolleys is just not done here.

Newport:

- If you must smoke a pipe, it can only be done during daylight hours.

Providence:

- You can avoid paying property taxes if you are disabled or poor.

- See-through clothing is not allowed.

- Toothpaste and a toothbrush cannot be purchased at the same time on Sundays.

Scituate:

- Beer is not allowed in the passenger area of a vehicle. It does not matter if it is open or closed.

The Wacky World Of Laws: 2nd Edition

SOUTH CAROLINA

Statewide:

- When a man promises to marry a single woman, she can force him to do it.

- If a locomotive scares your horse, they could be fined.

- Once establishing itself in any town of over 500 people, a railroad cannot stop serving a town.

- Telling fortunes requires a state license.

- On Sundays, you can only dance at home.

- You cannot buy a banjo on Sunday. The state has nothing against banjoes. They prohibit the sale of all musical instruments.

- Tattoos are considered tacky and illegal.

- Livestock over a certain size cannot be kept in a bathtub.

- Alcohol is only available in private clubs on Sundays.

- Committing an involuntary murder while attempting suicide can get you the death penalty.

- Minors cannot play coin-operated gaming machines.

- Cosmetologists need more hours of formal training than law enforcement officers.

- Do not go to a barber school if it does not have at least ten barber chairs.

- The fourth Friday in October is "Frances Willard Day." All schools are required to have a program discussing the problems relating to alcohol on this day.

- Circuses can only spend so much time in the same place.

- Any restaurant which offers "frozen dessert" must specify exactly what this dessert is.

- A jealous legislator must have been involved in this act. It is illegal for a married man over 20 to engage in a private discussion with a married woman over 50.

Charleston:

- If they think it is required to prevent a conflagration, the fire department can destroy your home.

- Most motorized vehicles have been outlawed on King Street.

Clemson:

- If your apartment swimming pool is open after 11 PM, it must have a lifeguard.

- Female dogs who are "in the mood" must not roam freely.

Fountain Inn:

- Horses appearing in public must be outfitted with appropriate pants.

Greenville:

- The sun must shine before liquor can be sold.

- The only people who can legally drink at Furman University are people who are at least, 60-years-old.

Hilton Head:

- Lots of trash in your car is illegal. *Actual Law: Sec. 9-1-113. Conditions affording food or harborage for rats. (a) It shall be unlawful for any person to place, leave, dump or permit to accumulate any garbage, rubbish or trash in any building, vehicle and their surrounding areas in the town so that the same shall or may afford food or harborage for rats. Any violation of this subsection shall constitute a nuisance. (b) It shall be unlawful and constitute a nuisance for any person to permit to accumulate on any premises, improved or vacant, or on any open lots or streets in the town, any lumber, boxes, barrels, bricks, stones or similar materials and permit them to remain thereon unless the same shall be placed on open racks that are elevated not less than eighteen (18) inches above the ground and evenly piled or stacked, so that these materials will not afford harborage for rats or violate any other provisions of this chapter.*

Lancaster County:

- Public dancing is prohibited.

Myrtle Beach:

- You cannot change out of, or into, your bathing suit in a public restroom unless you get permission first. *Actual Law: Sec. 5-13. Changing clothes in public lavatories, etc. It shall be unlawful for any person to undress or to put on a bathing suit, change from a bathing suit to normal clothes or change from normal clothes to a bathing suit in any public lavatory or toilet room in the city without obtaining permission or consent from the •owner or proprietor.*

Spartanburg:

- To maintain a certain level of propriety (and avoid the seeds) you may not eat watermelons, or other picnic fare, in the Magnolia Street cemetery.

SOUTH DAKOTA

Statewide:

- Falling asleep in a cheese factory is prohibited.

- For quite some time, movies which showed law enforcement getting abused were illegal.

- No horses are allowed into Fountain Inn unless they are wearing pants.

- Even if you are raped, you cannot have an abortion in this state.

- It is illegal to try to convince a pacifist to renounce his beliefs by threatening to arm wrestle him.

- Every hotel room must have twin beds two feet apart and intercourse cannot be had in the space between the beds.

TENNESSEE

Statewide:

- You are not required to work on any of your religion's holidays. *Actual Law: (Constitution of the State of Tennessee-Article Xl Miscellaneous Provisions-Sec. 15. Religious holidays.: No person shall in time of peace be required to perform any service to the public on any day set apart by his religion as a day of rest.)*

- Some time ago, people of different races were not allowed to get married. *Actual Law: - Constitution of Tennessee - Article Xl: Miscellaneous Provisions: Section 14 (The intermarriage of white persons with negroes, mulattoes, or persons of mixed blood, descended from a negro to the third generation inclusive of their living together as man and wife in this State is prohibited. The legislature shall enforce this section by appropriate legislation.)*

- Every living animal, except for humans, qualifies as a "dumb animal." *Actual Law: 39-3-101 Definitions. -- In this part, and in every law relating to or affecting animals, the words animal or dumb animal shall be held to include every living creature; the words torture, torment, or cruelty shall be held to include every act, omission, or neglect whereby unjustifiable physical pain, suffering, or death is caused or permitted; but nothing herein shall be construed as prohibiting the shooting of birds or game for the purpose of human food, or the use of animate targets by incorporated gun clubs.*

- More than eight unmarried women living in the same house was not advised since it met the definition of a brothel.

- At one time, Ministers were prohibited from serving in the State Legislature. This was considered to be inappropriate for "men of God."

- You cannot be elected to public office if you have been in a duel.

- Daring a minor to illegally purchase alcohol is just as illegal as purchasing it for them.

- Driving while asleep is not only a bad idea, it is also illegal.

- Using a rope to catch fish is not allowed.

- Eating road kill is not only unsanitary, it is prohibited.

- Keeping a skunk, except for a certified zoo, is not permitted.

- Selling hollow logs is not allowed.

- Juveniles are not allowed to get tattoos.

Dyersburg:

- Women cannot call a man to arrange a date.

Fayette County:

- You cannot keep more than five non-running vehicles on your property without having a junkyard permit.

Kimball:

- Imitating loud parrot sounds, or any other annoying noises, is not allowed in a place which serves beer. *Actual Law: 8-105 Prohibited conduct or activities by beer permit holders It shall be unlawful for any beer permit holder to: (1) Allow any loud, unusual, or obnoxious noises to emanate from his premises.*

Knoxville:

- Hitching posts are required in front of most businesses.

Memphis:

- An old law, which may still be on the books, required a man to carry a red flag and precede a woman driving a car. This was to warn other people on the road.

- Boisterous frogs, or any form of animal, are not allowed after 11 PM.

- In order to beg in downtown, a person must get a license.

- Any leftover pie cannot be removed from a restaurant.

Nashville:

- Cheetahs, and most other exotic animals, are not allowed as pets.

- Roller skaters, roller bladders, or skateboarders cannot attach themselves to any other moving vehicle.

- Roller skating while listening to an iPod or Walkman is illegal.

- Groups of people riding mopeds must line up in single file.

TEXAS

Statewide:

• Some Texans would have you believe that all discussions about the state or its government must include one of these words: big, bigger, biggest goddamn, extra-large, giant, humongous, large, tall, tallest, or widest.

• You can find the alleged law on many internet listings: "when two trains meet each other at a railroad crossing, each shall come to a full stop, and neither shall proceed until the other has gone."

• Treating a corpse with disrespect (cursing, exposing yourself, etc.) is just plain rude, as well as illegal.

• Adding graffiti to livestock which does not belong to you is wrong.

• You cannot milk someone else's cow unless you work for them.

• Owning more than a certain of "intimate satisfaction devices" is illegal.

• Once, there was a law which prohibited publishing methods on how to make "home brew.' If this is correct, then the Encyclopedia Britannica could be banned.

• Taking someone else's garbage could get you in trouble, even if you are hungry.

• Horseback riding at night might require the use of red reflectors.

- Operating a sidewalk vending stand requires a license. This makes most lemonade stands illegal.

- Adultery can be prosecuted if one party complains.

- Rain making is strictly regulated in this state.

- Donating body parts is allowed. Selling body parts is not.

Abilene:

- Hanging out to find chicks, or for "flirting or mashing" is illegal.

Austin:

- Carrying concealed wire cutters is prohibited.

Beaumont:

- Lamar University banned football.

Borger:

- Be careful what you throw here. The following items (just a few of a long list) are not allowed: cactus fruit, confetti, feather dusters, fireworks, riding crops, or whips.

Clarendon:

- Keep your feather dusters at home. They are not welcome in public buildings.

Commerce:

- Stay off of telephone poles, unless you work for the phone company.

Corpus Christi:

- Raising alligators as a home enterprise is prohibited.

Dallas:

- It is not allowed to own "personal massage devices" which look like human body parts.

Dennison:

- Women are not allowed to adjust their stockings in public. It is considered too provocative.

El Paso:

- Women are not allowed to appear in an "indecent or lewd dress."

- Spittoons are required in most public facilities or meeting rooms.

Galveston:

- Keep your camels, and other wild critters, properly restrained.

- Walking or standing is allowed. Sitting on the sidewalk is illegal.

- Driving on local beaches has been allowed for some time. Landing an airplane, except during an emergency, is not allowed.

- Another warning for pilots: do not dump your trash out while flying.

- Consuming alcohol in a city park is only allowed when you have a permit.

- Bicycles can only be run at "acceptable speeds".

Harker Heights:

- Swearing in church might be a sin. It is certainly illegal if it disturbs the parishioners.

- It took a specific law to remind city workers that they must obey all traffic laws.

Houston:

- Special offers related to beer are strictly regulated.

- Many items, including limburger cheese, could not be sold on Sunday.

Lubbock County:

- In some areas, having an open container of alcohol in a vehicle is legal. Here, alcohol must be kept out of reach of the driver.

Mesquite:

The Wacky World Of Laws: 2nd Edition

- Children's hair must not be cut in such a manner as to cause a disturbance.

Plano:

- It is interesting to ponder why this law was created. You cannot sell foam alligators at parades in this town.

Port Arthur:

- Watch your vapors here. Emitting foul smelling scents in an elevator is both rude and illegal.

Richardson:

- No "U turns" are allowed here.

- Parking your car on the street for the purpose of selling it, or placing a for sale sign in it which is visible from a public road is prohibited.

San Antonio:

- Flirting with your hands or eyes is banned.

- It must be due to a water shortage, because having multiple toilets in your home is prohibited.

Temple:

- Riding a horse in a saloon is OK, if the floors are suitable.

Texarkana:

- Horseback riding after dark might require special lights attached to the horse's behind.

UTAH

Statewide:

- Riding a horse and fishing are not allowed at the same time.

- During an emergency, alcohol sales are not allowed.

- Having a beer larger than two liters is prohibited.

- If you cause a "catastrophe," you can go to jail.

- According to some people, you are legally required to drink milk.

- Like most states, exploding a nuclear device is illegal. However, you might be able to legally have one with you.

- Vehicles must yield the right of way to birds.

- Before a restaurant can serve you wine, you must specifically ask for it.

- Making whoopee in the back of an ambulance while on an emergency call is illegal.

Kaysville:

- It does not matter how old you look, everyone entering a convenience store after sunset is carded.

Logan:

- Women must watch their tongues. Inappropriate language is not permitted.

Provo:

- The operation of shaved ice stands is severely restricted here. They are prohibited between November 1 and April 30.

- No snowball throwing is allowed.

Salt Lake County:

- You can only do so much to let the public know you are having an auction. Some prohibited things are the use of trombones and cursing. *Actual Law: 5.54.310 Unlawful activities designated. All auctioneers are forbidden to conduct their sales in such manner as to cause people to gather in crowds on the sidewalks so as to obstruct the same; nor shall they use immoral or indecent language in crying their sales, or make or cause to be made noisy acclamations such as ringing of bells, blowing of whistles, or otherwise, though not enumerated here, through the streets in advertising their sales; and no bellman or crier, drum or fife or other musical instrument or noisemaking means of attracting the attention of passersby, except the customary auctioneer's flags, shall be employed or suffered to be used at or near any place of sale or at or near any auction room, or near any auction whatsoever.*

- Carrying a violin in a paper bag in public could be suspicious. The police might want to talk with you.

Tremonton:

- Getting caught while having sex in a moving ambulance has some interesting forms of punishment. The man gets off scot-free. The woman's name is printed in the local newspaper.

Trout Creek:

- You cannot legally treat headaches with gunpowder.

VERMONT

Statewide:

- A woman cannot get false teeth without her husband's permission.

- Tying a giraffe, or any other exotic animal, to a telephone pole is not allowed.

- At one time, it was illegal to be an atheist.

- Painting landscapes during wartime was thought to be a waste of paint.

- Wasting paint in order to paint a horse is also prohibited.

- It's against the law for vagrants to procure food by force in this state.

- It is illegal to defame a court here as well.

- Whistling under water is illegal.

Barre:

- The official bath night is Saturday. Everyone has to participate.

Rutland:

- Do not let your car backfire. It is considered a disturbance.

VIRGINIA

Statewide:

- The legal reason for being in a cemetery is to visit people buried there.

- Once upon a time, having an indoor bathtub was illegal.

- Unless you want a trip to jail, do not have sex until you are married. *Actual Law: Virginia Code 18.2 344 states, "Any person, not being married, who voluntarily shall have sexual intercourse with any other person, shall be guilty of fornication, punishable as a Class 4 misdemeanor."*

- In accordance with the preceding law, the "missionary way" is the only way.

- The only people who can legally bribe someone during an election are the politicians.

- The raccoon is the only animal which can be hunted in Sundays, according to an old law.

- It is often said that you must wear shoes to legally operate a vehicle.

- Tickling a woman can get your face slapped, and you slapped with a citation.

Culpepper:

- If you must wash your mule, or any other livestock, keep it off the sidewalk.

Frederick:

- A special license is required to sell such things as coins and flatware.

Lebanon:

- While you may not like what she does, you cannot literally kick your wife out of bed for eating crackers, or for any other reason.

Norfolk:

- Seagulls must be treated with respect. Therefore, do not spit on them.

- Touching a woman in a place she does not want to be touched can get you jail time.

- During non-daylight hours, women must be accompanied by a man, and wearing a corset, according to an old law which might still be on the books.

Prince William County:

- You cannot keep a skunk, a giraffe, or a tarantula, among many others, as a pet. *Actual Law: Sec. 4-69. Definitions. For purposes of this article, the following words and phrases shall have the meanings respectively ascribed to them by this section: Animal shall include any live vertebrate creature, domestic or wild, not to include birds. Pet shall mean any animal kept for pleasure rather than utility. Vicious animal shall mean any animal or animals that constitute a physical threat to human beings or other animals but shall not include guard dogs. Wild or exotic animal shall mean any live monkey (nonhuman primate), raccoon, skunk, wolf, squirrel, fox, leopard, panther, tiger, lion, lynx or any other warm-blooded animal, poisonous snake or tarantula which can normally be found in the wild state or any other member of crocodilian, including but not limited to alligators, crocodiles, caimans, and gavials. Ferrets, nonpoisonous snakes, rabbits and laboratory rats which have been bred in captivity and which never have known the wild shall be excluded from this definition.*

- Residents cannot use profanity when talking about someone who is not present.

Richmond:

- Flipping a coin, or any other game of chance, cannot be done to decide who pays for a meal.

Stafford County:

- At one time, with adequate provocation, a man could beat his wife if they were on the courthouse steps during daylight hours. This is most likely "case law."

Virginia Beach:

- You can be arrested for DUI if you and the driver are both drunk.

- Bicycle handlebars are not intended as a place to sit.

- Watch your tongue when you are on the boardwalk, or on Atlantic Avenue. Cursing is not allowed there

WASHINGTON

Statewide:

- Lollipops have been banned.

- One old law says you cannot buy meat on Sundays.

- Painting polka dots on the American flag is not allowed.

- You cannot sell mattresses on a Sunday.

- An old law says motorized vehicles must have an escort. During daylight, it must be someone with a red flag. A night, a person with a red torch must walk in front of the vehicle.

- As part of an effort to deceive people, you cannot say you parents are rich, if they are not.

- Breast feeding was once outlawed.

- If for some reason, you feel you must attach a vending machine to a utility pole, you must get the utility company's permission.

- Being in public with a cold is not legal.

- No one is allowed to dispose of someone else's beer unless it is obvious they are through drinking it.

- It is illegal to try to lure girls away from the Maple Lane School for girls.

- Although it was once a common practice, you are not allowed to use X-ray machines to see if shoes fit properly.

Auburn:

- "Deflowering a virgin can get you some serious jail time in this town even if you are married to them.

Bellingham:

- Single-use plastic carry out bags are prohibited

Bremerton:

- Eating peanuts and throwing the shells on the street is not legal.

Lynden:

- No business may offer both dancing and drinking at the same time.

Seattle:

- Having a concealed weapon over six feet long is prohibited.

- A woman cannot sit on a man's lap on a public conveyance. She may sit on a pillow which is on his lap.

- If you want to burn down someone's outhouse, or any of their other property, you must first get their permission.

- Plastic straws are now prohibited.

The Wacky World Of Laws: 2nd Edition

Spokane:

- There is no swimming here, even if you have a life jacket. *Actual Law: Listing 10.19.010 Swimming in River. A. No person may intentionally enter, swim, dive, or float, with or without a boat, raft, craft, or other flotation device, in or upon the water of the Spokane River at any point between the east line of the Division Street bridge and the west line of the Monroe Street Bridge. B. The chief of police may, in accordance with procedures and criteria the chief may from time to time prescribe, grant permits for a person or persons to be in that portion of the Spokane River known as the forebay, being the south channel between Havermale Island and the south bank. C. The fact that a person is wearing or in possession of swimming, diving, or flotation gear or equipment on the bank of the river in the prohibited portion is sufficient ground for an arrest for attempt under this section and shall be prima facie evidence of intent.*

- You cannot buy a television or a radio on a Sunday.

- Strippers must stay at least four feet from all non-strippers.

Waldron Island:

- Each home is limited to a maximum of two toilets. This is according to San Juan County Ordinance NO. 7 - 1995, Passed June 7, 1995.

Wilbur:

- Riding an ugly horse is not considered proper or legal in this town.

Wacky Case:

In 2007, Jane Balogh registered her dog to vote. Her purpose was to highlight how easy it was for anyone to get registered. After attempting to get state legislators and government officials to respond to her complaints, Balogh decided this was the best way to get their attention. Using a utility bill address to her dog (Duncan M, MacDonald), she sent in an absentee voting application. Not wishing to actually vote, she used her dog's paw print instead of signing the application.

In court, where she finally got her chance to address the subject in public, Balogh said she wanted to make officials realize how easy it would be for non-existent people to register to vote. This also applied to undocumented people from foreign countries. She told the judge her intent was not to vote, but to make more people aware of the problem.

The judge allowed her to do ten hours of community service and pay a paperwork fee instead of giving her a much steeper possible fine. It was apparent that Balogh was not trying to violate voting laws.

WEST VIRGINIA

Statewide:

- You can get in trouble for making fun of someone who does not duel. *Actual Law: 612-24. Taunting for nonparticipation in duel; penalty. If any person post another, or in writing or in print use any reproachful or contemptuous language to or concerning another, for not fighting a duel, or for not sending or accepting a challenge, he shall be guilty of a misdemeanor, and, upon conviction, shall be confined in jail not more than six months, or fined not exceeding one hundred dollars.*

- If you decide to duel someone, you are disqualified for public office. *Actual Law: 6-5-7. Disqualification by dueling. Any citizen of this state who shall, either in or out of the state, fight a duel with deadly weapons, or send or accept a challenge so to do, or who shall act as a second, or knowingly aid or assist in such duel, shall ever thereafter be incapable of holding any office of honor, trust or profit in this state.*

- Red or black flags are outlawed. *Actual Law: 61-1-6. Display of red or black flag unlawful. It shall be unlawful for any person to have in his possession or to display any red or black flag, or to display any other flag, emblem, device or sign of any nature whatever, indicating sympathy with or support of ideals, institutions or forms of government, hostile, inimical or antagonistic to the form or spirit of the constitution, laws, ideals and institutions of this state or of the United States.*

- Wild onion breath is not acceptable among school children.

- Co-habituation and lewd association while unmarried can get you jail time.

- To insure better rail service, a law was passed which required railroads to serve communities of over 100 people if their tracks were within one mile of the town.

- There is a special tax for cola drinks.

- Sneezing on a train could make you a public nuisance.

- Keep your hats in the car if you go to an indoor theater.

- Road-kill is fair game.

Huntington:

- Women passing a fire station will not be flirted at by firefighters according to a local law.

Nicholas County:

- Ministers are not allowed to tell funny stories as a part of their sermon.

Peewee:

- Eating onions, or other produce, is prohibited at the local cemetery.

WISCONSIN

Statewide:

- Taking pictures of rabbits is only legal from January through April.

- Men are not supposed to cut women's hair.

- State prisoners are only allowed to eat butter. No artificial spreads are allowed.

- In order to prevent over-flushing, a law says that manual toilets are prohibited in new structures.

- Public displays of affection (PDAs) are not allowed on trains, and other public conveyances.

- Rape was once listed as "a man having sex with a woman that he knows is not his wife".

- Farm animals have the right of way on highways.

- Pharmacists were once required to keep condoms out of public view.

- It is often seen on the internet that one has to order their apple pie with cheese in this cheese producing state.

Brookfield:

- Tattoos are prohibited unless it is done to assist medical personnel.

• You cannot let someone use your phone to make immoral phone calls.

Hudson:

• All windows must have screens installed between May and October 1.

• Do not put your garbage in someone else's can unless they say it is okay.

• Do not sit in someone else's car without their permission.

Kenosha:

• Men are not allowed to have any visible sign of being "in the mood" while in public.

La Crosse:

• Horses cannot be hitched up on Third Street.

• Except for the period when they are being changed, all store window mannequins must be clothed.

Milwaukee:

• You cannot hire a fife and drum band to gather a crowd for your business.

• It is illegal to be "physically offensive" in public.

• Fireworks are illegal, machine guns are legal.

Newcastle:

- Do not even think about making whoopee inside a meat freezer in this town.

Racine:

- Don't wake up sleeping firefighters.

- Unescorted women may not walk down a public road at night.

St. Croix:

- Women wearing red are not allowed here.

Sun Prairie:

- The construction of nuclear weapons is prohibited here.

- Your hands must always be on your handlebars when bicycle riding.

- Cats are not supposed to hang out in cemeteries.

- Keep the snow off your property or face a fine.

Wauwatosa:

- Either your books or your library card must remain in the library.

- Water fountains are for beauty, not swimming.

- Anyone who twists the truth in order to get a meeting room will face harsh judgment.

WYOMING

Statewide:

- There is a special sales tax on targets which look like one of the Clintons. You can get a tax deduction for purchasing an automatic weapon.

- Mining is dangerous enough without being drunk. Being drunk in a mine can get you're a healthy fine.

- Being drunk is not allowed when doing business with a junk dealer.

- Keep that extra-large cowboy hat at home when you go to the theater. The people behind you have the legal right to see the stage.

- Fishing with a firearm is prohibited.

- Don't let the cows get out. Leaving the gate open is not allowed here.

- Drunk Skiing is also a violation of the law.

- Art is considered important here. One publication says you are required to spend at least one percent of your construction budget on artwork for any building which costs more than $100,000.

- In Yellowstone Park, the personal hygiene products a woman should wear around bears are strictly regulated. *Actual advisory from the National Park Service: "Considering bears' highly developed sense of smell, it may seem logical that they could be attracted to odors associated with menstruation. Studies on this subject are few and inconclusive. If a woman chooses to hike or camp in bear country during menstruation, a basic precaution should be to wear internal tampons, not external pads. Used tampons should be double-bagged in a ziplock type bag and stored the same as garbage."*

Cheyenne:

- Citizens may not take showers on Wednesdays.

The Wacky World Of Laws: 2nd Edition

FEDERAL LAW

- 40 USC §1315 & 7 CFR §502.11 makes it a federal crime to bring your unvaccinated pet to the Beltsville Agriculture Research Center in Beltsville, Maryland.

- 7 USC §8303, §8313 & 9 CFR §93.318(b) makes it a federal crime to bring an American horse back into the United States after being in a Canadian rodeo without a health certificate.

- 47 USC §509(a)(3) makes it a federal crime to engage in a scheme to prearrange the outcome of a knowledge-based game show on broadcast television.

- 7 USC §7734 & 7 CFR §319.41–1(b)(2) & 319.41–6 makes it a crime to mail mature corn on the cob into the United States from Canada (west of and including Manitoba) without a permit for the corn cob mailing.

- 27 USC §§205(e), 207 & 27 CFR §5.42(a)(8) makes it a federal crime to receive hard liquor in interstate commerce if its label falsely says that drinking it will be therapeutic.

- 7 USC §§4912(a) & 4908(c) makes it a federal crime for a department of agriculture employee to reveal how a watermelon handler voted in a watermelon referendum.

- 16 USC §470ee(b)(2) & 32 CFR §229.3(a)(3)(vi) makes it a federal crime to buy mummified human flesh taken from public land, if it's at least 100-years old.

- 16 USC §1540 & 50 CFR §17.40(b)(1)(i)(B) makes it a federal crime to kill a grizzly bear in self-defense without reporting your self-defense killing within 5 days.

- 15 USC §1254, 16 CFR §1500.18(a)(8) & 1511.3(b) makes it a federal crime to sell a baby pacifier without at least two vent holes in it.

- 21 USC §§1037(b)(1), 1035, 1041 & 9 CFR §590.560(c) makes it a federal crime for an egg handler to handle eggs while they have a communicable disease in a transmissible stage.

- 26 USC §5687 & 27 CFR §31.202(a) makes it a federal crime to possess a liquor bottle that has been refilled with liquor since it was originally filled.

INTERNATIONAL LAW

Australia:

- A light bulb can only be changed by certified electricians.

- Internet modems are not allowed to connect on the first ring.

- You cannot wear pink "hot pants" after noon on Sundays.

Bermuda:

- The maximum speed limit is 20 m.p.h.

- Tourists cannot rent cars to drive themselves.

- In almost all occasions, suitcases are not allowed on buses.

- There is a maximum vehicle length for cars of a little over 14 feet.

- Most household are limited to one automobile.

- The modesty police will contact any woman wearing a dress which starts more than eight inches above the knee.

- Halter tops are not allowed on women in public.

Bolivia:

The Wacky World Of Laws: 2nd Edition

- A woman can be a prostitute as long as she does not look for customers in public places.

- One glass of wine, or alcoholic beverage is the most a single woman is allowed to drink in a public restaurant or bar.

- A man cannot engage in an intimate relation with both a woman and her mother.

Cambodia:

- Due to a problem of spreading infections from tainted water, New Year's revelers cannot squirt people with water guns.

Canada:

- How you pay for things is important here. If you use only pennies, the maximum is 25 cents. If you use nickels, the maximum is $5. For dimes, it is $10.

- If you listen to Canadian radio, you'll notice that every fifth song is by a Canadian citizen. This is not a fluke. It is the law.

- Encrypted broadcasts are illegal unless they are approved by the government. So, unapproved encrypted satellite channels are illegal.

Chile:

- Until 2004, divorce was illegal under almost all circumstances. It was circumvented by pretending that you were not actually one of the people listed on the original marriage certificate.

Valparaiso:

- A woman who has been convicted of adultery cannot get married.

China:

- You must prove you are intelligent before you can go to college.

- Vehicles which stop at pedestrian crosswalks can face a fine.

- Citizens can only have one child or heavy fines can be imposed.

- Rescuing a drowning person is prohibited since it would interfere with their fate.

- The ancient and once popular practice of foot binding to keep a female's feet from growing is now illegal.

- Imperial law once imposed death for anyone who disclosed the secret of how silk was made.

- In China it seems to be legal to engage in cannibalism. But you can't deliberately consume the flesh of another man's wife. Because that would be rude. Eat your own wife, that is politer.

- In the Chinese province of Guizhou there is a new law attempting to reduce road traffic accidents. They took a strange approach, making it law that all children must stop and salute a car whenever one drives past. It's a weird one, but apparently, it actually works in reducing road accidents.

• In the Chinese county of Gongan, there was a really strange law up until recently. It stated that all local government employees were required to buy and smoke at least 23 thousand packets of cigarettes each year. It was shortly overturned again as almost anyone can see its flaws. One of the biggest flaws is that the cost of all those cigarettes far exceeds the average pay of a Chinese government worker. So, it really didn't make sense. It didn't make sense at all. But the law was introduced to support local cigarette sellers.

Denmark:

• Based on a sad situation while someone was trying to find a problem, you are not allowed to start the motor on a car while a mechanic is underneath it.

• A simple glass of water must be free at restaurants. Adding ice, a twist of lime or a sprig of mint allows you to charge extra.

Ecuador:

• For a woman to legally dance in public, she must have some fabric covering her navel. There are no limitations on what other parts MUST be covered.

England:

• England has lots of old laws which have not been repealed. For example, if a young man is under 14 years old, he must devote two hours a day to learning how to properly use a long bow.

- If you have the plague, taxi drivers do not have to serve you.

- With proper provocation, and after 9pm, you may beat your wife, if it does not disturb your neighbors.

- In a law dating back to the early 1300s, wearing a suit if armor into Parliament is illegal for members of the peerage.

- Dying within Parliament is also prohibited.

- Public display of drying laundry is illegal.

- Commerce on Sundays was strictly limited. However, you could buy carrots.

- To show how picky royalty could be, this is a law dating back many years. "Any person found breaking a boiled egg at the sharp end will be sentenced to 24 hours in the village stocks."

- Another case of "Royalty has its privileges" is that any dead whale that washes up on a beach belongs to the King and/or Queen. They are the only ones who can legally profit from it, or by it.

- Postage stamps bearing the likeness of the King or Queen must always be applied to a letter right side up.

- Christmas Day is not the correct day to eat a mince pie.

- Scottish custom, and law, requires that you must allow a stranger to use your toilet, if they ask you politely.

- The needs of pregnant women are heeded in this empire. If nature calls, she can relieve herself in any convenient facility. This includes using a police officer's hat.

- Daylight hours are the only time Welch men are allowed within the city limits.

- The only woman who can work topless in Liverpool is a clerk in a store which sells tropical fish.

- If you need to transport a corpse or a rabid dog, do not expect a taxi to stop for you.

- Carrying a bow and arrow in York, and being from Scotland can get you killed within the old part of this town.

Finland:

- The ability to read is a requirement for a marriage license.

- Illegal parkers get the air let out of their tires here.

- Animated characters must wear clothes. Because of this, Donald Duck was not seen for some time.

France:

- No porcine animal can be named Napoleon.

- Public displays of affection are often prohibited on trains.

- Dolls are only allowed to have human faces.

- To protect their national treasure of wine, a law was passed which made it illegal for any flying machine, including UFOs, to land in a vineyard.

Germany:

- Running out of gas on the autobahn is not only dangerous, it is illegal.

- In some circumstances, a pillow is considered a weapon.

- Every person who works in an office must be positioned is such a manner that they can see some part of the sky.

Greece:

- Playing games on a computer in a public place is not allowed.

- Keeping your driver's license requires a good working knowledge of the driving laws. It also is required that you dress properly and are clean.

Guinea:

- The name Monica has been banned under almost all circumstances, for unknown reasons.

Iceland:

- You do not have to have a medical degree to practice medicine here. As long as you display a sign which reads "Scottulaejnir" you can open a clinic. That word translates as "quack doctor."

- Before any building is built, the land must be proven to be free of elves.

India:

- Cheating on tests is not taken lightly here. If you are caught, you can go to jail even if you are 15 years old.

- In 1860, a new law made adultery illegal. However, only the man can be jailed.

Iran:

- Zoos should not encourage sexual activity by lions.

- Eating snake meat on a religious day is not acceptable.

- It has been reported that more than 100 criminal violations can get you executed.

Israel:

- Unauthorized radio stations are illegal. However, if you get away with it for over five years, you can legally keep broadcasting.

- Pig farming is strictly limited in this country.

- Getting dressed or undressed should be done in the dark.

- Skirt wearing men can spend time in jail.

- It might be some sort of tax law, but you are required to take your receipt with you when you leave a café.

- Several centuries ago, a "labor of moles" was cited for causing excessive damage to crops. They were ordered to appear in court. When they failed to do so, they were officially exiled from the country.

Italy:

- A law in Venice states that all gondolas not belonging to government authorities be painted black.

- Smiling in Milan is both acceptable and legally expected most of the time here.

Laos:

- Displaying your toes in public is not allowed.

Madagascar:

- Wearing a hat while you are pregnant is not allowed.

Malaysia:

- Toilet paper should not be used instead of a napkin in a public eating establishment.

Mexico:

- While riding a bicycle, both feet must be on the pedals.

- Public cursing is not allowed in Guadalajara and neither is wearing provocative clothing in government offices.

New Zealand:

- Being married has its benefits. A married couple can drink alcohol at the age of 18. Single people cannot legally drink adult beverages until they are 20.

Norway:

- Female dog and cats cannot be spayed. Male dogs do not get this consideration.

Peru:

- Not wanting the prisoners to start acting in a "spicy" manner, hot sauces are not allowed in prison foods.

- You can keep a female alpaca in your home, unless you are an unmarried young man.

Russia:

- Driving a dirty car can get you in trouble.

- You cannot purchase food for livestock at a bakery. (Article 152).

- The Council of Ministers of the RSFSR announced that signs posting any information other than material related to public safety are illegal along roadways.

- Do not bother foreigners. Actual Law: Article 164.3, pestering foreign citizens for the purpose of acquiring things is prohibited.

Qatar:

- Being pregnant and unmarried limits your medical options to almost nothing. Either you treat yourself, or leave the country.

Doha:

- A naked woman is expected to cover her face first if she is surprised by an unexpected visitor.

San Salvador:

- Drunk drivers could face execution.

Singapore:

- You are required to flush the toilet after each use.

- Repeat litter offenders are required to clean the streets while wearing a sign which says you are a litterer.

- Public busses are not the place to chew gum.

- Smoking in public, along with feeding the birds, is not allowed.

South Korea:

- Any effort to bribe a police officer will be immediately reported to their supervisors.

- Recently, the South Korean legislature passed a law requiring that all bloggers and chat room participants provide verifiable identification. No more anonymous postings.

Spain:

- Several decades ago an Alsatian breed of dog was jailed because it kept stealing purses from women.

- Spain had to pass a law to insure than men did half of the housework.

Sweden:

- In an expression against animal cruelty, seals cannot be trained to balance anything on their noses.

- Residents cannot change the color of their home without a license.

- A Swedish monarch who marries someone without the civil government's permission can cause their heirs to lose their right to the monarchy.

Switzerland:

- A bomb shelter must be in close proximity to every Swiss citizen.

- Slamming a car door can be considered disturbing the peace.

- Long ago in a Swiss court, a rooster was determined to be the "Devil in disguise" when it was found that he unnaturally laid an egg despite being male.

- A man can only legally look at the body of his wife.

Thailand:

- You must wear a shirt while driving in this country.

- Underwear is also required if you are going to be in public places.

- Citizens can get a fine for stepping on the nation's paper money, as it often has a photo of the King.

- Taxi drivers must be prepared for many things. This includes always carrying a body bag which could hold a body which weighs up to 265 pounds.

Turkey:

- It is considered taboo to make fun of modern Turkey's founder: Ataturk.

- Fights among fans of different male belly dancers became so frequent that authorities eventually banned all such dances by men.

ABOUT THE AUTHORS

About Jeff Isaac, The Lawyer In Blue Jeans

Jeff Isaac, Esq., AKA "The Lawyer in Blue Jeans," is the founder and principal attorney at The Lawyer in Blue Jeans Group, a San Diego law firm dedicated to providing high quality legal services delivered in a straight-forward manner. The firm provides many services, including the establishment of Revocable Living Trusts, Trust and Probate Administration, and Business Entity Formation.

Jeff's San Diego based law firm addresses a distinct niche within the legal profession by providing consumers with affordable services that take a proactive approach to help shield against lawyers, legal fees, courts, and the related emotional and financial costs.

Jeff is an energetic hybrid of pragmatic legal advice, humor, and insightful commentary on life's daily legal challenges. With over 40-years of experience as an attorney, he offers down-to-earth expert perspective on both personal legal issues as well as those current events in law that affect San Diego society on a day-to-day basis. Jeff's distinctive style of what he calls "Blue Jeans Law" is highly relatable and comforting to a public that is known to harbor negative misconceptions about attorneys at large.

In today's overly litigious society, this "Blue Jeans Law" philosophy is a welcome and refreshing view of the legal system with the "common man's" interest at heart. Jeff can relate to his audience, due to his background as a High School Football Coach, Member of the Judge Advocate Generals Office in the Army, as well as his consistent involvement in charity and community events.

Jeff is an invigorating public speaker and media personality, with unique style and a light-hearted perspective for radio and television. Listeners benefit from candid discussions about the legal issues that affect their daily lives. As a sought-after cross-media expert source, Jeff appeared weekly on XETV Channel 6 in San Diego for several years, where he served as a legal expert, providing insightful legal explanations, interpretations, and perspective on legal issues.

About Justin Isaac, Attorney at Law

Justin Isaac has worked at the Lawyer in Blue Jeans Group for eight years. He received his Juris Doctorate from Thomas Jefferson School of Law in 2016.

Justin has extensive knowledge of estate planning and takes personal accountability in ensuring that each clients' needs are met. He is committed to carrying out the Lawyer in Blue Jeans Group's philosophy of delivering sensible and reliable service. In addition to helping clients with their estate planning needs, Justin also offers legal advice weekly on the radio. He can be heard on Sunday's at 9 a.m. on 760 KFMB AM with Attorney at Law, Jeff Isaac, where they discuss legal news and advise callers who have questions about their own personal legal matters.

Justin was born and raised in San Diego where he currently resides. When he is not assisting clients with their legal needs, he enjoys watching soccer, playing golf, and traveling.

www.ingramcontent.com/pod-product-compliance
Lightning Source LLC
Chambersburg PA
CBHW060832220526
45466CB00003B/1077